JANE AUSTEN *in* BATH

Walking Tours of the Writer's City

KATHARINE REEVE

The Little Bookroom ✦ *New York*

For Alex and Thea

© 2006 Katharine Reeve

Design by Louise Fili Ltd

Cover: The Crescent, from "Bath Illustrated by a Series of Views," engraved by John Hill (1770-1850) published by William Miller, 1804, after John Claude Nattes (c.1765-1822) / Private Collection, The Stapleton Collection/Bridgeman Art Library

Library of Congress Cataloging-in-Publication Data

Reeve, Katharine

Jane Austen in Bath : walking tours of the writer's city/Katharine Reeve.

p. cm.

Includes bibliographical references and index.

ISBN 1-892145-32-4 (alk. paper)

1. Austen, Jane, 1775-1817--Homes and haunts—England—Bath. 2. Novelists, English—Homes and haunts—England—Bath. 3. Novelists, English—19th century—Biography. 4. Walking—England—Bath—Guidebooks. 5. Literary landmarks—England—Bath. 6. Bath (England)—Intellectual life—19th century. 7. Bath (England)—In literature. I. Title.

PR4036.R44 2006

823'.7—dc22

[B]

2006010832

Printed in China

The Little Bookroom

1755 Broadway, Fifth floor

New York, NY 10019

(212) 293-1643; (212) 333-5374 fax

editorial@littlebookroom.com

www.littlebookroom.com

CONTENTS

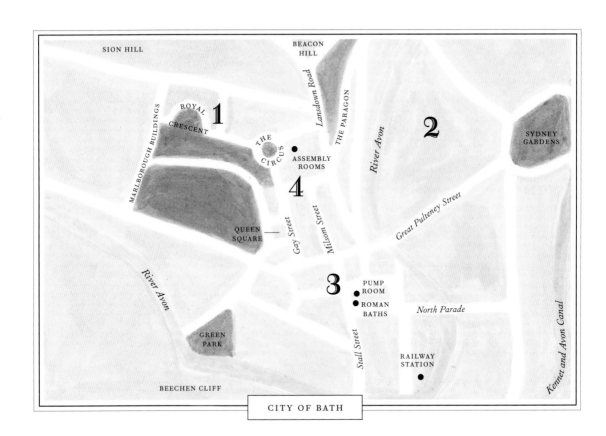

CITY OF BATH

INTRODUCTION

T HE CITY OF BATH ROSE TO PROMINENCE IN THE EIGHTEENTH CENTURY AS A CENTRE OF FASH-
IONABLE ENGLISH SOCIETY, SECOND ONLY TO LONDON FOR THE SOPHISTICATED PLEASURES
it offered. Centuries earlier the Romans had discovered natural thermal springs there and created a settlement
known as Aquae Sulis; the health-giving properties of these same springs later drew Georgian pleasure-seekers
and invalids to Bath. The city became a magnet for royalty, the nobility, gentry, and the new affluent industrial
classes, who in turn attracted writers, musicians, and artists seeking patrons and a market for their work. The
city's dramatic architecture, high fashion, and social extravagance attracted visitors from all over Europe including Charles Dickens, Thomas Gainsborough, Joseph Turner, Tobias Smollet, Fanny Burney, Horatio Nelson,
Joseph Haydn, and Franz Liszt.

Jane Austen made her first two visits to Bath in November 1797 and in May 1799. Her family had strong ties
to the city: Jane's mother's relatives had connections there and it was where Jane's parents had met. For families
like the Austens, Bath was a more affordable and socially accessible alternative to London.

THE MAKING OF BATH
By 1800 the once ramshackle rural town of Bath had spread well beyond its medieval walls, and its population

had reached thirty-two thousand. Much of this transformation had taken place early in the eighteenth century, the result of the vision of four men: businessman Sir Ralph Allen; architects John Wood the Elder and the Younger; and Richard "Beau" Nash. Allen owned the quarries that provided the limestone used for building in Bath. In 1727 he commissioned the architect John Wood the Elder, recently returned to the city from Italy, to transform the muddy streets and shabby wooden buildings into a gleaming, neoclassical Palladian showpiece. Wood the Elder proceeded to lay out a new street plan, houses, and public buildings that would result in a truly modern city with unique buildings such as those of the Royal Crescent and Circus.

Allen realised that buildings alone would not improve Bath's fortunes; the city needed to entice a "better class of visitor." He encouraged Beau Nash, an opportunist and inveterate gambler, to invigorate Bath's social life and entertainments. Nash established dances and card rooms, and helped to expand the city's famous theatre. As Master of Ceremonies, he developed strict behaviour and dress rules that were advertised in all public rooms and enforced firmly.

By 1750, Bath had become *the* place to go for the winter season, which ran from October to May. At the city's peak of popularity, more than twenty thousand visitors would arrive each year. An army of increasingly wealthy physicians would be on hand to deal with disease and winter illnesses; meanwhile, polite society could be entertained and allowed to make advantageous alliances. For fifty years Bath enjoyed rapid growth and prosperity built on tourism. It was not until later in the century that its fortunes slumped, when royal whim dictated a shift in fashion to new seaside resorts such as Brighton.

JANE AUSTEN'S EARLY YEARS

After George Austen and Cassandra Leigh's marriage in 1764, they moved to the village of Steventon in the rolling countryside of Hampshire, where Mr. Austen, a clergyman, had been asked to oversee two parishes. Their second daughter, Jane, was born on December 16, 1775, at Steventon Rectory. Her father welcomed her as "a present plaything for her sister Cassy and a future companion." Cassandra was three years older than Jane, and as Mr. Austen predicted, they were to be the closest of companions throughout their lives.

Their home was a large rectory with a wildflower-lined footpath from the house to the church. The elm, chestnut, and fir trees that Jane loved stood alongside the house. Life at home was intellectually stimulating and boisterous—Jane and Cassandra had five brothers. Jane's childhood was one of noisy home theatricals, energetic games in the garden, and helping her mother around the house. She received little formal education and spent only brief stays away from home being taught in small schools with Cassandra.

At a time when the education of women was the subject of much debate, women of the gentry often had to make do with self-education by making use of their father's libraries. They were often given lessons from private tutors or family members in French and Italian, painting, needlework, poetry, music, and dancing, but they were usually discouraged from studying the more "masculine" subjects of Latin and mathematics.

In *Pride and Prejudice*, Mr. Bingley considers women accomplished so long as they can "paint tables, cover skreens, and net purses." His sister proposed that to be truly accomplished "a woman must have a thorough knowledge of music, singing, drawing, dancing, and the modern languages, to deserve the word." Yet Jane had observed that "a woman, especially if she has the misfortune of knowing anything, should conceal it as well as she can" (*Northanger Abbey*).

In Jane's case, however, extensive reading was encouraged by both parents and facilitated by Mr. Austen's large, up-to-date library. Jane was familiar with well-known eighteenth-century writers including Samuel Johnson, Mary Wollstonecraft, Tobias Smollett, Ann Radcliffe, and Fanny Burney and she enjoyed lively debates about their merits with friends and family. At age twelve, Jane decided to devote all her spare time to writing. By the age of twenty-four she had written three novels: *Sense and Sensibility*, *Pride and Prejudice*, and *Northanger Abbey*.

Jane's life spanned a turbulent period in English history: the US War of Independence, the French Revolution, industrialisation and urbanisation, and the Napoleonic Wars. Her novels offer insights into the social history of England as it transformed itself into a modern nation with a new and increasingly wealthy "middling" class that would ultimately wrest power from the aristocracy. The influence of the French Revolution was felt in the early nineteenth century, when rising social consciousness combined with food shortages led to calls for reform. Despite moves towards equality for certain groups, women were still largely dependent on fathers, husbands, and brothers for their financial security, and they had little intellectual freedom or formal education and certainly no role in public life.

COUNTRY AND CITY

The Austens' social life in rural Hampshire revolved around their small circle of friends and family. Many of Jane's lifelong friendships—with the Bigg-Wither sisters, Madame Lefroy, and Martha Lloyd—date from these years. As there were no shops in the village, Jane and Cassandra would make trips to nearby Andover and Alton to buy paper, ink, and fabric for dresses. Dances and parties were held regularly at the Assembly Rooms in Basingstoke, seven miles away.

England was becoming increasingly urbanised during the late eighteenth century, and Jane used the distinction between city and country to good literary effect. In her novels the city becomes a place of disappointment and of deception, and her city characters often exhibit artifice, deceit, indolence, vice, meanness, and bad manners. Criticism of the countryside instantly marks a character unfavourably (as would a lack of interest in books): the hardened Mary Crawford of *Mansfield Park* exposes her true self when she mocks the "sweets of housekeeping in a Country Village." Conversely, country characters such as Catherine Morland, Anne Elliot, and the Dashwood sisters are shown to be generally trustworthy, generous, healthy, friendly, and moral. They also tend to be keen readers and walkers, pursuits that immediately identify the heroes and heroines of the novels.

JANE AUSTEN AND BATH

Although Jane's characters are precisely drawn, the settings in her novels are often vague, with the exception of Bath, which she grew to know intimately. It is the only urban setting she used and it was the focus of two of

Portrait of Jane Austen

her six published novels. The two Bath novels represent Jane's very different experiences of the city: *Northanger Abbey* introduces an innocent young girl, Catherine Morland, enjoying a holiday there in the late 1790s, whereas *Persuasion*'s world-weary Anne Elliot feels imprisoned there, resigned to a lonely spinsterhood and forced to live in a city that by 1814 was past its prime.

Jane's own stable, happy life in the countryside was interrupted in spring 1801 when Jane, Cassandra, and their parents suddenly left Steventon to live in Bath, where they remained until summer 1806.

As far as Jane's private life is concerned, the Bath years are something of a mystery. Letters from the period 1801–1806 were mostly destroyed, and little evidence remains. What we do know is that she was deeply shocked by the sudden nature of the news that she would be leaving her childhood home and that she may have fallen into a depression in the years that followed, causing an abrupt break in her writing. Alternatively, she might have made the best of life in Bath and been simply too busy to write, with increased household chores, distractions, and regular trips away.

This book explores Bath as Jane knew it: as a young visitor, as a resident, and as a writer, following her along the streets she walked, to the areas she lived in, the places she visited, shopped, and portrayed in her novels.

Katharine Reeve
BATH

Detail of Manuscript page from Persuasion

THE NOVELS OF JANE AUSTEN

Sense and Sensibility, begun 1795, published in 1811

Pride and Prejudice, begun 1796, published in 1813

Mansfield Park, begun 1811, published in 1814

Emma, begun 1814, published in 1816

Northanger Abbey, begun 1798, published in 1818

Persuasion, begun 1815, published in 1818

The Watsons, begun 1804, unfinished

Sanditon, begun 1817, unfinished

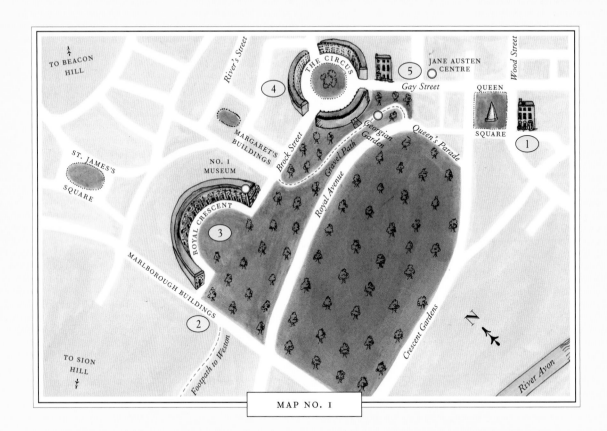

MAP NO. I

WALK 1

Jane's First Visits to the Georgian City of Bath

View of Bath, 1805

JANE'S FIRST VISITS TO THE GEORGIAN CITY OF BATH

"They arrived at Bath. Catherine was all eager delight—her eyes were here, there, everywhere, as they approached its fine and striking environs, and afterwards drove through those streets which conducted them to the hotel. She was come to be happy, and she felt happy already." (Northanger Abbey)

THE FIRST VIEW OF BATH, AS YOU COME OVER THE HILLS THAT SURROUND IT, IS AS ARRESTING NOW AS IT WAS WHEN JANE AUSTEN LIVED THERE IN THE EARLY 1800S. THE POET Robert Southey described Bath, with its rows of tall white limestone terraces snaking their way up and down the slopes, as the "finest and most striking town I have ever seen." An earlier visitor, Katharine Plymley, a Shropshire artist and naturalist, recorded her impressions in her journal in 1794:

I am extremely struck by the beauty & singularity of Bath. Passing through Queens Square, up Gay Street to the Circus & Crescent, I am ready to suppose that I am not in England. The uniformity of building, all of stone, the breadth of the flags [stone pavement], the openings everywhere into the country, shewing the hills that surround the town scatter'd over with stone houses in all situations, everything is new, & the streets remind me of views I have seen of the insides of towns in Italy.

The creator of Georgian Bath, John Wood the Elder, would have been delighted by the comparison. Inspired by his Grand Tour to Italy, he hoped to build an English version of Carthage. For eighteenth-century visitors, Bath, with Wood's dramatic set pieces of Queen Square, the Royal Crescent, the Parades, and the Circus, was brand new and dazzling to the eye. The city's unusual architecture, uncommonly clean and orderly streets, and glittering social scene made it like no other town in the land.

Two main reasons brought visitors to Bath in the eighteenth century: the health-giving properties of the waters of the ancient spa and the lively social life of the season. For a young woman such as Jane Austen, used to living in the countryside, where entire villages could be isolated during the long winter months and entertainments were sparse, a trip to the fashionable city of Bath would have been a source of considerable excitement.

Bath was one of the few cities with a fast coach service to and from London (about one hundred miles away) and other towns in nearby counties, including Jane's home town of Steventon, seventy miles distant. The journey itself was a source of trepidation; roads were frequently impassable in winter, and sudden summer rainstorms could wash away the road's surface. Highwaymen, who lay in wait for coach parties, presented another hazard to travellers. Only the wealthy had their own coaches; Jane's family used the public ones.

Jane visited the city in 1797 and again in 1799 before moving there in 1801. She first stayed at the invitation of her aunt and uncle, Jane and James Leigh-Perrot, with her mother and sister. The Leigh-Perrots spent every winter season at their townhouse in Bath. Her second visit was a more luxurious holiday with her wealthy elder brother Edward and his family.

For a novelist, the attractions of Bath were great. The city offered a microcosm of Georgian society, and in this Jane found real-life models for many of her fictional characters: the obsequious Mr. Collins; wealthy, sought-after young men like Mr. Bingley; headstrong young girls like Lydia Bennet from *Pride and Prejudice*; the opportunistic Crawford siblings from *Mansfield Park*; beautiful but penniless young women such as Marianne Dashwood in *Sense and Sensibility*; and a wide variety of military men on leave.

Jane was twenty-three years old at the time of her second visit to Bath. Her brother Edward and his wife planned to be there for the last month of the summer season in May 1799 and invited Jane and Mrs. Austen to stay with them and their young children, Fanny and Edward. Jane's brother had inherited a vast fortune in 1797 from his adoptive parents, the Knights, who were the childless cousins of Mr. Austen. It was usual for wealthy, childless couples to ensure that estates remained in family hands by choosing a particular boy of the family as an heir. The Austens, who were not wealthy, would have seen the obvious benefits of this arrangement. Edward had inherited the estates of Godmersham in Kent, in addition to Chawton Estate in Hampshire, with an income of five thousand pounds a year.

This more leisurely visit meant that Jane could observe the Bath season properly from the comfort of Queen Square, one of the city's best addresses. Her deeper knowledge of the city and its social life would find its way into *Northanger Abbey*, which she had already started writing.

As the century drew to a close, Jane was drifting into an increasingly precarious position as an unmarried young woman with little to offer in the way of a dowry. *Pride and Prejudice*'s Mr. Collins pointed out that time was growing short for Elizabeth Bennet, whose "portion is so small that it will in all likelihood undo the effects of loveliness and amiable qualifications." Only men such as Mr. Darcy, with fortunes of their own, could choose to take a penniless bride, but only after conquering almost insurmountable obstacles placed in the way by members of their own family. Time and again Jane shows couples prevented by their families from marrying, usually for want of money. In *Persuasion*, Anne Elliot and Captain Wentworth are forced apart because he did not have a sufficiently impressive position and income; only years later, once he is sufficiently well off, would they be allowed to marry.

In 1795, Jane had fallen in love with one Tom Lefroy, who would later go on to be Chief Justice of Ireland, but his family removed him from the area before any understanding about marriage to Jane could be reached. As they were about to part, Jane confided in her older sister Cassandra, "I am to flirt my last with Tom Lefroy, and when you receive this it will be over. My tears flow at the melancholy idea" (January 15, 1796). Cassandra had resigned herself to early spinsterhood following the death in 1797 of her fiancé of five years, Thomas Fowle. It was the need of money for marriage that had sent him to the West Indies, where he contracted a fatal disease. Jane was no doubt thinking of their recent losses when she wrote: "Friendship is certainly the finest balm for the pangs of disappointed love" (*Northanger Abbey*).

Bath was notorious as a marriage market; the arrivals listing in the newspaper was filled with the names of single women. Robert Southey, writing in 1803, summed up the situation when he said that Bath was perfect for disreputable men who "make it their business to get a wife of fortune, having none themselves; age, ugliness and idiocy being no objections." Jane portrays fortune hunters of both sexes: the determined Crawford siblings, Henry and Mary, in *Mansfield Park*, and the financially embarrassed General Tilney and the unsophisticated John and Isabella Thorpe of *Northanger Abbey*. Jane's portrayals of patronised spinsters, such as Miss Bates in *Emma*, leaves no doubt that theirs was a state to be avoided. In an 1817 letter to her niece, Fanny Knight, Jane wrote, "Single Women have a dreadful propensity for being poor."

Though she considered various potential suitors over the years and received one serious marriage proposal, Jane remained unmarried, true to her belief that "anything is to be preferred or endured rather than marrying without affection." She was also clear about the negative aspects of marriage; exhausted by constant childbearing, women of her day had no real control over their destinies. Jane would have read Mary Wollstonecraft's *Vindication of the Rights of Women* (1792) with empathy, but it was still her father and later brothers who negotiated with publishers, and on whom she relied for survival.

Queen Square, looking west, 1784

STOP 1 ❧ QUEEN SQUARE

I like our situation very much; it is far more cheerful than Paragon, & the prospect from the Drawingroom window, at which I now write, is rather picturesque, as it commands a prospective view of the left side of Brock Street, broken by three Lombardy poplars in the garden of the last house in Queen's Parade. (May 17, 1799)

JANE ARRIVED IN BATH ON FRIDAY, MAY 17, 1799. SHE IMMEDIATELY WROTE TO CASSANDRA: "WELL, HERE WE ARE AT BATH; WE GOT HERE ABOUT ONE O'CLOCK, & HAVE BEEN ARRIVED JUST long enough to go over the house, fix our rooms, & be very well pleased with the whole of it…It has rained almost all the way, & our first view of Bath has been just as gloomy as it was last November twelvemonth."

After a brief stop at her uncle's house at No. 1 the Paragon, where, despite a raised pavement, it was too muddy to get out of the coach, Jane and her mother headed further into the centre of the city to 13 Queen Square, where they were to stay. By the time they pulled up outside the tall corner house they had already seen three people they knew—such was the small world of Bath society. The house was large and well positioned, facing the Royal Crescent and the Circus to the north, and was close to the luxury shops of Milsom Street and the restorative cures of the Pump Room and Baths.

Queen Square, built between 1728 and 1736, was the first part of John Wood the Elder's new scheme for Bath. Wood built an ostentatious mansion for himself on the north side of the square, directly opposite Jane's drawing room window. Jane soon settled at a table in front of the large window overlooking the square to write to Cassandra. As she peered at the streets below, she wrote of her hopes that the afternoon would be brighter: "When we first came, all the umbrellas were up, but now the Pavements are getting very white again."

Jane's first day at Queen Square was spent reading the local papers. She reported that "there was a very long list of Arrivals here in the newspaper yesterday, so that we need not immediately dread absolute Solitude—& there is a public breakfast in Sydney Gardens every morning, so that we shall not be wholly starved." The Austens pored over the arrivals section of the paper, which provided a list of royalty, aristocracy, gentry, and other visitors of note. To be included in this listing meant that one had status on Bath's social circuit. It also alerted those compiling guest lists as to who was in town.

Jane's letters to Cassandra during this visit are full of gaiety and wit. Charged with the task of bringing back a fashionable sprig to decorate Cassandra's bonnet, Jane kept her sister up to date on the progress of this trifling shopping quest:

> *Flowers are very much worn, & Fruit is still more the thing.—Eliz: has a bunch of strawberries, & I have seen Grapes, Cherries, Plumbs, & Apricots—There are likewise Almonds & raisins, French plumbs & Tamarinds at the Grocers, but I have never seen any of them in hats.*

Jane and Cassandra, as unmarried daughters, spent long periods apart because they were first in line for family duties, such as helping during the confinements of their sisters-in-law and caring for sick relatives. This resulted in a constant exchange of letters. Conscious of the cost of postage, Jane made maximum use of the paper by turning it ninety degrees and writing across the existing lines, a common practice of the time. There are about 150 remaining as a record of her thoughts, and there would have been many more had it not been for the assiduous editing and burning by Cassandra, to whom Jane had entrusted her letters in her will.

To protect reputations, it was common at the time for those in the public eye to burn their personal correspondence when approaching death. Cassandra destroyed many letters and struck out passages in others with heavy black ink, so there are key gaps around the Bath years, and no diaries survive to compensate. Jane's true feelings about her life in Bath and any short-lived romantic attachments remain a mystery.

Leave Queen Square at the northwest corner into Royal Avenue, turn right (where you can see the old sedan chairmen's waiting area) and then onto the gravel path (laid out in 1771). This allows wonderful views of the western side of Bath and glimpses into the gardens of the Circus and Brock Street, one of which can be visited. Leave the path before you reach the Royal Crescent and walk through the park towards Marlborough Buildings and tiny Cow Lane, which Jane walked along to start her walks to Weston over Sion Hill.

Marlborough Street, 1805

STOP 2 ❧ MARLBOROUGH BUILDINGS

I spent Friday evening with the Mapletons, & was obliged to being pleased in spite of my inclination. We took a very charming walk from 6 to 8 up Beacon Hill, & across some fields to the village of Charlcombe, which is situated in a little green Valley, as a Village with such a name ought to be. (June 2, 1799)

MARLBOROUGH BUILDINGS, ADJACENT TO THE ROYAL CRESCENT AND FACING CRESCENT FIELDS, WAS A DESIRABLE ADDRESS MUCH USED BY MEMBERS OF THE GENTRY FOR ACCOMmodation during the season. It bordered the fields, which contained a well-worn path—reached through Cow Lane, a gap in Marlborough Buildings—often used by visitors for long evening walks.

Jane enjoyed the quiet of the beautiful countryside surrounding Bath. Walking was one of her favourite activities, and her novels are full of the characters' favoured walks. Evening walks were popular in Bath and were generally prearranged by groups of keen walkers. Jane's Queen Square address was the perfect starting point for either gentle strolls up the gravel path to the Royal Crescent or longer country rambles.

Jane laced up her sturdy ankle boots then walked north, along the western side of the square, cutting through an opening to Queen's Parade, then past the waiting stands of the sedan chairmen on Queen's Parade Place, soon reaching the gravel path that would take her up the winding route to the Royal Crescent. Halfway, the grandeur of the Crescent loomed into view and the church at Weston could be seen clearly to the west of the city. Fifteen years later, Jane evoked this regular walk when writing the final romantic scene in *Persuasion* where, after many years apart, the hero and heroine finally declare their love for each other and "slowly paced the gradual ascent, heedless of every group around them, seeing neither sauntering politicians, bustling house-keepers, flirting girls, nor nursery-maids and children."

For longer, more energetic outings, Jane walked through a gap in the Marlborough Buildings, across the fields to Sion Hill, following a popular rural path towards the pretty village of Weston (now linked to the city by Victoria Park and terraced housing of the Victorian period). Alternatively, she struck out to the northeast along city streets and Lansdown Road for the climb to the heights of Beacon Hill. In *Northanger Abbey*, Jane has the stylish Eleanor Tilney introduce Catherine to the pleasures of walking in and around Bath. There follows a detailed description of the arduous walk undertaken by the young heroine and her new friends to the top of Beechen Cliff, "that noble hill whose beautiful verdure and hanging coppice render it so striking an object from almost every opening in Bath."

While men were expected to race about the countryside on horseback, for most women of the gentry, exercise consisted of promenading along scenic parades and squares. Dancing was possibly the only acceptable form of energetic physical activity for women, and we know from her letters that Jane was an accomplished and enthusiastic dancing partner. In polite society, evidence of exertion was considered unbecoming in a lady, and a flushed face, mud on a hem, or any form of wild "country" behaviour was frowned upon. For both Jane and Catherine Morland, however, coming from country families with many brothers, physical rough-and-tumble was what they were used to as children, and the habit was not altogether curbed by adulthood. Jane's sophisticated cousin Eliza de Feuillide had noted on an earlier visit to the Austens' house that, although the Austen sisters were delightful, their manners were unpolished.

Walk along Marlborough Buildings towards the Royal Crescent, stopping halfway along at the Royal Crescent Hotel.

The Royal Crescent, 1777

STOP 3 ❧ ROYAL CRESCENT

A fine Sunday in Bath empties every house of its inhabitants, and all the world appears on such an occasion to walk about and tell their acquaintance what a charming day it is. (Northanger Abbey)

VISITORS FROM ALL OVER EUROPE CAME TO MARVEL AT THE UNIQUE WORK OF JOHN WOOD, FATHER AND SON. THE ROYAL CRESCENT, BUILT BY JOHN WOOD THE YOUNGER BETWEEN 1767 and 1775, was the first open curved terrace in Britain and inspired many other crescents in Bath and elsewhere. Building these tall, dramatically sweeping crescents on the steeply sloping hills radiating from the medieval centre was a stunning feat of engineering. When finances allowed, Wood's approach was to level sites. Later architects built along the slopes of streets of such as Lansdown Road and Camden Crescent, following the natural curve of the land rather than attempting to flatten out the sites. They introduced deep vaults underneath the street level, which became shallower in houses furthest up a hill, and they adjusted decorative details, such as cornices on the façades to create the illusion of unified design.

The thirty houses of the Royal Crescent quickly became the residence of first choice for royalty and the upper echelons of society. At £3000 each in 1795, they were by far the most expensive houses in Bath. A house of similar size in Great Pulteney Street cost £2000, and in the lower town £1000.

The central, elegantly furnished house at 16 Royal Crescent, with a coach house and stabling for sixteen horses, was home to the Duke of York, King George III's second son, in the late eighteenth century. (This house is now the Royal Crescent Hotel, and the stables have been converted into a restaurant at the rear of the house beyond the tea garden.) To create the grand interiors of these houses, master craftsmen used the latest designs from fashionable pattern books. These can still be seen at 1 Royal Crescent, which was one of the first houses on the Crescent to be built and is now a museum (see p. 128). It has been carefully restored using eighteenth-century materials and period furnishings.

Walk east along the Crescent to No. 1, then walk along Brock Street, the Tilneys' route home from walks on the Royal Crescent, pausing at Margaret's Buildings, where you can see all that remains (a doorway) of the small Georgian Margaret Chapel, bombed in World War II. Continue along Brock Street to the Circus.

STOP 4 ❧ THE CIRCUS

EVEN THE BEAUTIFUL PRINTS OF BATH'S FAMOUS LANDMARKS COULD NOT PREPARE THE VISITOR FOR THE SPLENDOUR OF THE CIRCUS, DESIGNED BY JOHN WOOD THE ELDER AND completed by his son, John Wood the Younger. It required the time-consuming and costly levelling of the sloping site to make way for this unique structure, built between 1754 and 1766. By 1768 all thirty-three houses were occupied. The Circus formed part of Jane's route around the city. Her friends, Marianne and Jane Mapleton, lived at No. 11, where she visited them many times.

The Circus consists of three terraces of tall narrow houses that curve around a central circular space whose diameter of 318 feet deliberately matches that of the stone circle of Stonehenge; Wood was fascinated by ancient English history and the druids in particular. The Circus was likened to the Colosseum turned inside out; its tiers of Doric, Ionic, and Corinthian columns echoed those of the ancient Roman monument. The façade is highly decorative—a carved frieze of more than five hundred images from the arts and sciences, sea and agriculture, runs around the top of the whole circle. The traditional English symbol of the acorn is present in the form of giant carved finials.

The Circus's central piazza was originally paved (the plan was to use it for sporting events), but by 1801 it had been replaced by a reservoir of water for household use surrounded by shrubbery. By 1829, trees were planted over the old reservoir, and it was their canopy of branches that trapped a Second World War bomb, sav-

The Circus, 1773

ing the Circus from certain destruction. The city was attacked over a couple of nights during spring 1942 in what became known as the Baedeker bombing campaigns (named after the travel guides because the Germans had targeted culturally prestigious sites). Many Georgian buildings in the city were damaged, including the southeast side of Queen Square and the Assembly Rooms.

Walk around the Circus clockwise, turning left into Gay Street and stopping outside No. 25, the house that Jane, her mother, and sister lodged at for a short time in 1805, taking a series of rooms.

Fanny Austen-Knight by
Cassandra Austen, c. 1810

STOP 5 ❦ GAY STREET

GAY STREET WAS ONE OF THE BUSIEST THOROUGHFARES IN BATH—FULL OF SEDAN CHAIRS AND PEDESTRIANS BUSTLING BETWEEN THE UPPER TOWN, QUEEN SQUARE, AND THE BATHS. Cheaper than many of the famous streets, it was a popular choice for doctors and lawyers who needed a convenient central address to receive clients. Jane used it as the location of Admiral Croft's lodgings in *Persuasion*, and for a few months in 1805 she herself lived here at No. 25.

The area around Gay Street and the Circus was populated by Bath's many artists, including Thomas Gainsborough. Visitors to Bath provided a livelihood for more than 150 artists. In the eighteenth century, all forms of portraits were in demand, from large, expensive canvases to affordable cut-paper silhouettes and miniatures, popular love tokens exchanged by engaged couples and intended to be worn next to the heart. Bath had a reputation as being the best place to find high-quality miniaturists. Numerous jewellery shops set the tiny pictures into lockets, bracelets, or small velvet frames into which plaited locks of hair could be placed. In *Persuasion*, Wentworth kindly offers to take a miniature portrait of Captain Benwick to be reset on behalf of his friend, Captain Harville. 40 Gay Street is now the Jane Austen Centre (see p. 128).

Walk down Gay Street towards Queen Square. No. 41, on the corner, was once the home of John Wood the Younger.

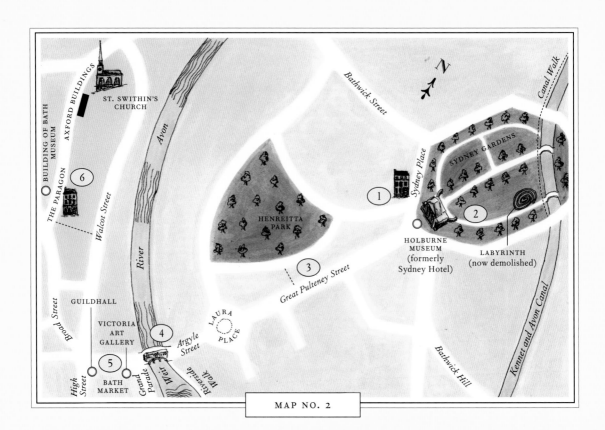

ST. SWITHIN'S
CHURCH

AXFORD BUILDINGS

BUILDING OF BATH
MUSEUM

THE PARAGON

⑥

Walcot Street

Avon

River

Bathwick Street

N

Canal Walk

SYDNEY GARDENS

Sydney Place

①

②

LABYRINTH
(now demolished)

HOLBURNE
MUSEUM
(formerly
Sydney Hotel)

HENREITTA
PARK

③

Great Pulteney Street

Kennet and Avon Canal

Bathwick Hill

Broad Street

GUILDHALL

VICTORIA
ART
GALLERY

⑤

High Street

BATH
MARKET

④

Grand Parade

Weir

Argyle Street

Riverside Walk

LAURA
PLACE

MAP NO. 2

WALK 2

The Move to Bath: Sydney Gardens and the New Town

STOPS

Sydney Gardens, 1805

THE MOVE TO BATH:
SYDNEY GARDENS AND THE NEW TOWN

I get more and more reconciled to the idea of our removal. We have lived long enough in this neighbourhood: the Basingstoke balls are certainly on the decline, there is something interesting in the bustle of going away, and the prospect of spending future summers by the sea or in Wales is very delightful…[It] must not be generally known, however, that I am not sacrificing a great deal in quitting the country, or I can expect to inspire no tenderness, no interest, in those we leave behind. (January 3, 1801)

DURING THE WINTER SEASON OF 1800 IN HAMPSHIRE, JANE WAS BUSY ATTENDING BALLS WITH HER FRIENDS MARTHA LLOYD AND THE THREE BIGG-WITHER SISTERS, ELIZABETH, CATHERINE, and Althea. The weather that winter was stormy and wet, making it difficult for those without a horse at their disposal to venture out. While staying with Martha, Jane complained to Cassandra (who was staying at Edward's home in Kent) that "it is too dirty even for such desperate Walkers as Martha & I to get out of doors, and we are therefore confined to each others society from morning till night, with very little variety of Books or Gowns."

Martha accompanied Jane back to Steventon in early December, just before Jane's twenty-fifth birthday on December 16. As their luggage was being taken upstairs by the servants Jane received a shock. Her niece, Caroline Austen, recalled her mother's version of events: "My Aunts [Jane and Martha] had been away a little while, and were met in the Hall on their return by [Jane's] mother who told them that it was all settled, and they were going to live at Bath. My Mother who was present said my Aunt Jane was greatly distressed—All things were done in a hurry by Mr Austen & of course this is not a fact to be written and printed—but you have authority for saying that she *did* mind it."

Despite fond memories of her visits to Bath, Jane had not expected to be uprooted from family, friends, and the countryside where she had grown up with the "privilege of country liberty, of wandering from place to place in free and luxurious solitude" (*Sense and Sensibility*). Jane loved Steventon, the Austens' seventeenth-century, seven-bedroom rectory surrounded by fields and formal gardens with a turf walk, strawberry beds, beehives, chickens, and pigs. It was the place that had inspired her to write.

Nevertheless, Mr. Austen, approaching seventy, had decided to retire as rector of Steventon and Deane parishes and pass this living over to his son James. Bath seemed a sensible choice to Mr. and Mrs. Austen. There they could enjoy retirement in one of England's most agreeable cities, free of the upkeep of a large house and the demands of parishioners. In 1801 residents of Bath enjoyed a high standard of living for considerably less money than in London. The design of the city's terraces gave the impression of grand mansions, but homes were in reality relatively small and required only a few servants. Since Bath was a small city there was little need for a coach and horses, and the staff they required. Bath was second only to London for the range of exotic comestibles available; food could simply be bought rather than produced at home.

Jane had been very clear when writing about Bath for the first time in *Northanger Abbey* that "though it is vastly well to be here for a few weeks, we would not live here." But as dependent daughters, Jane and Cassandra had no choice but to move with their parents. That Christmas, the move was the focus of all discussion in the various Austen family households across the southeast of England, but none of the letters sent by Jane that December survived.

By January 1801, her composure recovered, Jane sent a stream of letters to Cassandra in Kent, detailing all the plans for the move, which had been set for early May. She prepared the contents of their Steventon home for distribution to relatives or for sale at the local auction house. Everything in the house, including personal papers and books, had to be recorded and decisions made about what to give away and what to sell. Ultimately the decision was made to leave behind her father's cherished library of more than five hundred books, as well as the pictures and Jane's pianoforte. Among the few things kept were the beds and Jane's mahogany writing desk, a gift from her father.

The home was to be taken over by Jane's brother, James, and his second wife, Mary Lloyd, Martha's sister. Jane pointed out to Cassandra, "Mary is more minute in her account of their own gains than in ours." Before the family had even left, Mary inspected the house, noting repairs and alterations to be made. This insensitivity may have inspired Jane's portrayal in *Sense and Sensibility* of the scheming Fanny Dashwood, who relished her own good fortune even though it left her husband's stepsisters almost destitute. Jane's experience adds poignancy to her portrayal in *Persuasion* of the two unmarried sisters, Elizabeth and Anne Elliot, who were forced to leave their home to move to Bath because their father had frittered away his fortune.

Sydney Hotel, 1805

STOP 1 ❧ SYDNEY PLACE

Entering Bath on a wet afternoon, and driving through the long course of streets from the Old Bridge to Camden-place, amidst the dash of other carriages…she persisted in a very determined, though very silent, disinclination for Bath; caught the first dim view of the extensive buildings, smoking in rain, without any wish of seeing them better. (Persuasion)

THE AUSTENS ARRIVED IN BATH IN TWO SEPARATE PARTIES, MUCH TO JANE'S DISAPPOINT-MENT, SINCE SHE WANTED TO TRAVEL WITH CASSANDRA. LEAVING STEVENTON ON MONDAY, May 4, 1801, she and her mother travelled with very different feelings about what lay ahead. Jane "did not speak above once in three miles" to her mother, who was looking forward to seeing her much-loved brother, James Leigh-Perrot, and his wife. They arrived in Bath at half past seven in the evening, and after a cup of tea, Jane retired to her room near the top of the house to set her things "very comfortable about me." The plan was for Jane and Mrs. Austen to house hunt from the comfort of the Leigh-Perrots' house on the Paragon, and for Mr. Austen and Cassandra to follow on a month later, ostensibly to prevent crowding in the house.

The sale of the contents of the house at Steventon had been announced in the local *Reading Mercury* for the first week in May. The family was anxiously waiting for news of the prices fetched, since they were relying on this to fund the fitting out of their new house. News of the sale eventually reached Bath, and on Tuesday, May 12,

Jane wrote to Cassandra about the "blow of only eleven guineas for the tables. Eight for my pianoforte is about what I really expected to get; I am more anxious to know the amount of my books, especially as they are said to have sold well." A few weeks later she was cross about the low prices offered: "Mr. Bent seems *bent* upon being very detestable, for he values the books at only £70. The whole world is in a conspiracy to enrich one part of our family at the expense of another."

A fashionable address was crucial to social success in Bath. *Persuasion*'s wealthy Lady Dalrymple and her daughter took the largest, most extravagant house in Laura Place for three months. Sir Walter predicted that "they will move in the first set in Bath this Winter." Each of the Austens had a favourite part of Bath: Mrs. Austen favoured the area around Queen Square. Gay Street would have been on the list but was not affordable. But Mr. Austen's preferences had evolved: "At present the environs of Laura Place seem to be his choice… He grows quite ambitious, and actually requires now a comfortable and a creditable-looking house."

Caught between her father's aspirations and her mother's equally unrealistic desire to be near Queen Square, Jane was losing hope of finding something suitable when she spotted an advertisement in the *Bath Chronicle* of May 21:

The lease of No. 4 Sydney Place,

3 years and a quarter of which are unexpired at midsummer. The situation is desirable, the Rent very low, and the Landlord is bound by contract to paint the first two floors this summer. A premium will therefore be expected.

Apply Messrs. Watson and Foremen, Cornwall Buildings, Bath.

Sydney Place was a brand-new gleaming white terrace opposite the Sydney Hotel and Pleasure Gardens. It was part of a grand project of tall houses overlooking a hexagonal garden developed in the early 1790s and designed by architect Thomas Baldwin. Jane had always secretly hoped for the leafy surroundings of Sydney Gardens, which she knew from the gala evenings she had attended in 1799. From the three tall windows of the drawing room on Sydney Place, Jane enjoyed unbroken views of meadowland. It was a perfect location for her parents since the magnificent Great Pulteney Street around the corner provided a level walk over the bridge to the markets and Pump Room.

Although Bath's elegant crescents, squares, and parades had been built long before Jane arrived, the city was still expanding. The new town, of which Sydney Place was a part, was built on the Bathwick estate on the eastern side of the river, owned by the influential and wealthy William Pulteney. For many years it resembled a building site, full of workmen, "vapour, smoke and confusion." Bath's speculative building boom of the early 1790s had nearly doubled the number of houses in the city, feeding the demands of thousands of visitors by creating vast crescents and terraces higher and higher up the slopes to the heights of Sion Hill, Lansdown, and Camden. The city was also opening out to the east, along the London Road and through the meadows of Bathwick.

The summer redecoration mentioned in the house advertisement fitted perfectly with the Austens' plans to go away to the South Devon coast. Knowing that Bath would be unbearably hot from June to early October, the family decided to make full use of the city's convenient location and plentiful coaches. Jane later wrote of Anne Elliot "dreading the possible heats of September in all the white glare of Bath."

On their return, Jane and Cassandra planned to finish the interior decoration themselves, taking advantage of Bath's excellent fabric, furniture, and print shops: "I flatter myself that for little comforts of all kinds our apartment will be one of the most complete things of the sort all over Bath, Bristol included."

Jane's first month in Bath was enlivened by a new friendship with a Mr. Evelyn, the cousin of a friend of Edward's whom she mentions meeting at a ball. In a letter to Cassandra she wrote: "I assure you in spite of what I might chuse to insinuate in a former letter, that I have seen very little of Mr Evelyn since my coming here; I met him this morning for the 4th time, & as to my anecdote about Sidney Gardens, I made the most of the Story because it came in to advantage, but in fact he only asked me whether I were to be at Sidney Gardens in the evening or not.——There is now something like an arrangement between us & the Phaeton, which to confess my frailty I have a great desire to go out in;—whether it will come to anything must remain with him." No more is known about her relationship with Mr. Evelyn, because her letters suddenly end there.

4 Sydney Place is not open to the public, but the biannual meetings of the Jane Austen Society are held here.

Cross the road to the Holburne Museum and Sydney Gardens.

STOP 2 ❧ SYDNEY GARDENS

It would be very pleasant to be near Sidney Gardens!—we might go into the Labyrinth every day."
(January 21, 1801)

I N OCTOBER 1801, THE START OF THE WINTER SEASON, THE AUSTENS FINALLY TOOK POS-SESSION OF THEIR HOUSE AT 4 SYDNEY PLACE. WITH ONLY A COOK, A YOUNG MAID, AND A manservant, the burden of family duties in the new house-hold landed on Jane and Cassandra. The number of servants one kept related directly to one's income; in *Sense and Sensibility*, Jane describes Mrs. Dashwood as pitied for her reduced circumstances of just a cook, "two maids and a man" to help at Barton Cottage.

Life there was noisy and full of activity. The house was on a busy corner, with a pub behind (the Pulteney Arms, still there today) and the "bawling of newsmen, muffin men & milkmen, and the ceaseless clink of pattens" on the pavements, which so annoyed Anne Elliot in *Persuasion*. (Pattens were inelegant, wooden-soled overshoes, essential in the winter months for those without a carriage to protect their boots from the muddy streets.) There was the regular clatter of carriages in and out of the carriage-entrance of the Sydney Hotel opposite, street-sellers knocking on doors throughout the morning, and the constant babble of passersby. Older women—such as Jane's mother, Mrs. Leigh-Perrot, *Northanger Abbey*'s Mrs. Allen, and *Persuasion*'s Lady Russell—relished the cheerful-ness and bustle of the city and felt that "these were noises which belonged to the winter pleasures" (*Persuasion*).

The bridges over the canal in Sydney Gardens, 1805

50

Now that they lived in a smaller house, Jane felt the need for regular escapes in the form of walks; either over the road to stroll through Sydney Gardens' tree-lined paths, or further afield into the countryside. Christopher Anstey's popular handbook to Bath described Sydney Gardens' "serpentine walks, which at every turn meet with sweet shady bowers furnished with handsome seats, some canopied by Nature, others by Art." He added that the Labyrinth with its many classical pavilions and swings was "twice as large as Hampton Court's." This allowed a walk of about half a mile through the maze.

The Gardens had been open for just six years by the time Jane took up residence opposite. They had been conceived as an exclusive, elegant meeting place for the "nobility and gentry" who, for a season's subscription fee of about eight shillings, would be given brass admission tokens embossed with a picture of the gardens. Adjacent to the gardens was the grand Sydney "Hotel," or tavern. Additional subscriptions were payable for card playing in the hotel's coffee room, and for reading the newspapers. Tea was sixpence and could be taken inside or delivered to a seat in the gardens. Jane enjoyed the popular Monday public breakfasts held outside in the specially designed dining booths in the gardens. These started at 10 AM and offered cold meats, cheese, eggs, bread rolls, and Sally Lunn tea cakes, with tea and coffee served at midday, followed by dancing till 3 or 4 PM. A ballroom had just been built at the hotel, as well as a separate tap or public house for servants, coachmen, and tradespeople, who were not allowed to mix with the gentry.

Royal birthdays provided occasion for grand galas. Visitors bought their two-shilling tickets in advance from local inns, libraries, or music shops. The festivities commenced at 5 PM with a supper of cold ham, chicken, rolls, wine, and porter (beer) served outside in the dining booths or, if the weather was cold, in the new banqueting room. This was the main venue for prestigious events, including, in September 1802, one of the first hot-air balloon flights by the Frenchman André Gamerin. Spectators had to pay handsomely for their tickets, but the excellent views from Jane's house were free. The city's location makes it perfect for ballooning, and on summer evenings in Bath one still can see the skies full of brightly coloured balloons.

Isambard Kingdom Brunel's Great Western Railway, one of the earliest railway lines in England, runs, unseen, through a deep cut made across the eastern side of the Gardens in 1840. This necessitated the destruction of the popular teahouse, Gothic castle ruin, and labyrinth. Although much reduced in size from Jane's day, the gardens still offer respite from the busy city, with tree-lined walks, grassy slopes, Georgian pavilions, and statuary.

The hotel in Sydney Gardens is now the Holburne Museum (see p. 128).

Exit Sydney Gardens alongside the Holburne Museum to the eastern end of Great Pulteney Street.

STOP 3 ❀ GREAT PULTENEY STREET

B Y 1800, GREAT PULTENEY STREET WAS ONE OF BATH'S MOST FASHIONABLE ADDRESSES; THE ALLENS OF NORTHANGER ABBEY RENTED ROOMS HERE. SIR WILLIAM PULTENEY, A LAWYER, was one of the richest men in England. He transformed the rural estate owned by his wife on the eastern side of the city into a new town, and he appointed Thomas Baldwin as estate architect in 1788. Moving away from the Palladian style favoured by Wood, Baldwin laid out an entirely new network of streets and houses inspired by Robert Adam's large-scale geometric designs. For this to be truly effective the streets had to be level. This was achievable on this sloping site only by building deep vaults under the high terraces of what was to be Great Pulteney Street. The gradual movement of the buildings over time can be seen most clearly in the distorted doorways and window frames of No. 22 and No. 33. This dramatically wide (one hundred feet) and elegant street lined with broad pavements and elegant classical façades was completed in 1792. This is the view that would have met Jane every morning as she turned the corner from her front door towards the markets and Milsom Street. One of the main advantages of life in Bath was that it offered Jane a certain amount of freedom to go out where and when she pleased. In the countryside she would have had to rely on lifts from her father or brothers to go shopping or to visit friends. Jane's daily route into town, along Great Pulteney Street, through Laura Place, and along Argyle Buildings to Pulteney Bridge was used in both of the Bath novels.

Great Pulteney Street from the Sydney Hotel, 1806

Walk to the end of Great Pulteney Street, across Laura Place, and into Argyle Street. On the left you will see the steps leading down to the riverside walk, just before you reach Pulteney Bridge. There are still shops lining this short decorative bridge, including one selling historic maps of Bath.

Pulteney Bridge, 1804

STOP 4 ❧ PULTENEY BRIDGE

FOR GREAT PULTENEY STREET AND SYDNEY PLACE TO EXIST, THERE FIRST HAD TO BE EASY ACCESS BETWEEN THE MEDIEVAL HEART OF THE CITY AND THE COUNTRYSIDE ACROSS THE River Avon to the east. The New Town's success hinged on the building of a major new bridge to replace the ferry service.

William Pulteney chose the highly fashionable architect Robert Adam to design the unusual shop-lined bridge overlooking the river façades. Adam was inspired by Palladio's unbuilt Ponte di Rialto in Venice. Controversy, mainly emanating from the all-powerful Bath Corporation, surrounded the project. The corporation claimed that Pulteney was dragging the modern city back in time by reviving medieval-style house-lined bridges known to cause street congestion. Nevertheless, the bridge was completed in 1774 with twenty shops ready for rent. Benjamin Ford's new ice cream shop at No. 13 placed an advertisement in the *Bath Chronicle* "offering ice creams for fourpence each, and plum and saffron cakes." At this stage the bridge led only to meadowland: the streets of one of Britain's most spectacular neoclassical architectural set pieces had yet to be built.

The severe storms of 1799–1800 caused such serious flood damage to Pulteney Bridge that the north side had to be rebuilt during 1802–1804. Walking along the southern side around the workmen, blocks of local limestone, and tools, Jane would have had a clear view of Beechen Cliff's tree-lined summit.

Residents spent many afternoons escaping the bustle of the city streets by disappearing down the tiny set of steps that led from the bridge to the leafy, muddy riverside path by the side of the weir. Walkers like Jane, and like the Tilneys and Catherine Morland of *Northanger Abbey*, could follow the curve of the river southwards past Widcombe, to the foot of Beechen Cliff and the steep ascent, which promised the finest views of the city.

By summer 1802 the cessation of hostilities between Britain and France brought the navy and army back home, filling the streets of Bath and Brighton with dashing officers, including Jane's brother Charles. He returned with presents of topaz crosses on golden chains for his sisters.

After a year in Bath, Jane's chances of finding a husband would still have been a regular topic of conversation for Mrs. Austen and Mrs. Leigh-Perrot. The pressure must have been great, because at Christmas 1802, while staying with the Bigg-Wither sisters, Jane accepted the unexpected proposal of marriage from their wealthy brother Harry Bigg-Wither, only to retract it the following morning. Jane and Cassandra, both upset and embarrassed, insisted on being driven to Bath immediately. In *Persuasion*, Anne Elliot refuses to marry an equally sensible choice, the local landowner Charles Musgrove. Neither Jane nor Anne Elliot could emulate the pragmatic Charlotte Lucas of *Pride and Prejudice* and marry without love.

At the end of the bridge you will see the Victoria Art Gallery straight ahead. Walk around the corner of the bridge onto Grand Parade, where you can see the impressive weir of the River Avon and Prior Park at the top of the hills to your left (straight ahead lies Beechen Cliff). Cross to the other side of Grand Parade to the Bath Markets entrance.

STOP 5 ❧ THE MARKETPLACE

A LARGE PART OF JANE'S DAILY ROUTINE REVOLVED AROUND THE EVENING MEAL. SHOPPING FOR FOOD WAS A RELATIVE NOVELTY FOR THE FAMILY, FOR AT STEVENTON EVERYTHING HAD been grown, slaughtered, cooked, and preserved by the Austens themselves. Now they had to come up with cash for everything. Because there was no refrigeration, food had to be bought fresh most days, with particular care taken over dairy products to avoid sour or "blue" milk, or bad butter.

Thanks to its demanding customers, Bath was one of the best food centres in the country. Its market, one of the oldest in England, expanded enormously during the eighteenth century. Stalls were housed in a covered building with separate areas for poultry, butter and dairy, meat, and vegetables. The market was renowned for its variety and inexpensive prices: according to *The Bath Guide*, "Fresh butter (equal to any in England) is brought in from the country every morning, and the butchers who live in the city supply the inhabitants with the best of meat every day of the week. The markets for fish are Mondays, Wednesdays and Fridays and are thought to excel those of any inland town." As *Northanger Abbey*'s Mrs. Allen noted, "There are so many good shops here. We are sadly off in the country…Here one can step out of the doors and get a thing in five minutes." Bath had grocery shops selling ready-made meals of savoury and fruit tarts, meat pies, cakes, cheeses, ham, pasta, Parmesan, olives, and ices, and there were countless bakeries and vegetable shops. Opposite the marketplace in a lean-to shop next to the Abbey (since demolished) was one of Bath's celebrated pastry-chefs, Gill. His competitor,

Town Hall, Markets, and Abbey, 1804

Mollands on Milsom Street (now a clothes shop), was Jane's favourite food shop and one of the only real shops to be featured in *Persuasion*.

There were frequent food shortages, false measures, and accusations of adulteration of foodstuffs (bread padded out with chalk, for example). To protect the market's reputation the Bath Corporation kept a close eye on the regulation of food and prices from its adjacent Guildhall weighing office. Bread prices were announced in the *Bath Chronicle* each week, and most people were keenly aware of ever-changing food prices. One of the first things Jane tells Cassandra about their new home concerns the cost of food.

I am not without hopes of tempting Mrs. Lloyd to settle in Bath; meat is only 8d. [pence] per pound, butter 12d., and cheese 9½ d. You must carefully conceal from her, however, the exorbitant price of fish: a salmon has been sold at 2s.[shillings] 9d. per pound the whole fish. The Duchess of York's removal is expected to make that article more reasonable—and till it really appears so, say nothing about salmon. (May 5, 1801)

Jane will have experienced the food shortages (and resulting price increases) of the early 1800s, mainly caused by a series of severe winters and bad harvests combined with the continuing wars. While England's rich powdered their hair with flour, the poor starved as the price of bread rose beyond the average daily wage of a labourer.

For the upper classes there were strict rules governing the timing of meals and the types of dishes to be served. The hour that dinner was served was an indicator both of fashionability and pretension, and Jane used it to great effect in *Northanger Abbey* to indicate her characters' social status. It was also a matter of practicality: the cost of candles would have been high for country families, so eating during daylight hours was more economical. At Steventon dinner would be at 3:30 PM, although at Edward's glamorous country house it would be late—at 6:30 PM; in town it would usually be between 5 and 6 PM.

French fashions dominated the preparation and cooking of imaginative meals. The style of serving dinner was also French-inspired: ten to twenty different savoury and sweet dishes, all meticulously arranged symmetrically around the table, would be laid out before guests in two courses. A large tureen of soup was always served; it might be the French-inspired White Soup (made of almonds, veal stock, and cream). For everyday family meals straightforward, old-fashioned English pease soup made of dried peas and vegetables was one of Jane's favourites. Large joints of beef and mutton, rabbit, pigeon pie, or whole fish would be accompanied by vegetables (from peas to beetroot cut into flower shapes), macaroni pie, savoury puddings, and sauces. Sweet dishes, which would prevail in the lighter second course, would include almond pudding, trifle, orange cheesecakes, and jellies, with fruit to follow. In the Austen home it is likely that, when not entertaining, the family would have five or six mixed dishes on the table in one serving, including meat and soup.

◆

No visitors appeared to delay them, and they all three set off in good time for the Pump-room, where the ordi-

nary course of events and conversation took place; Mr. Allen, after drinking his glass of water, joined some gentlemen to talk over the politics of the day and compare the accounts of their newspapers; and the ladies walked about together, noticing every new face, and almost every new bonnet in the room. (Northanger Abbey)

The Georgian day in Bath revolved around the two main meals of breakfast and dinner, and the evening's entertainments of the theatre, concert, cards, or dancing. Breakfast was usually served at ten o'clock and consisted of toast, honey, and Bath buns with tea (which Jane preferred) or coffee. Breakfasts for special occasions or before long journeys were more substantial. Mrs. Austen described one such feast of "Chocolate, coffee and tea, Plumb-Cake, Pound Cake, Hot rolls, Cold Rolls, Bread and Butter."

The round of the day's visits would start at about 11 AM and run until about 4 PM. During the early hours of the day servants walked briskly across town delivering visiting cards and invitations, all of which required immediate responses. A morning visit to the Pump Room was also on the list of activities for the day.

Church service was from noon till 1 PM, with evening prayers before 5 PM. Jane and her family attended regularly, sometimes twice in one day, favouring certain preachers and the churches to which they had subscriptions. Everyone would be home in time to change for dinner. At the turn of the nineteenth century, the main meal of the day was eaten very early between 3:30 (when natural light was still available) and 6 PM. In Bath dinner was generally just for immediate family; socializing took place after eating. Because her father and elder brother were in the clergy, Jane's life was infused by religious observance, and her novels reflected this in the number of clergymen featured and their generally sympathetic treatment.

Evenings were often organised around tea parties, with tea and cold snacks and sweet treats such as caraway cake and pyramid creams served at about seven o'clock. People attended the theatre or concerts, stopping later at the Assembly Rooms for dancing, tea, and mixing with a wider group of people. Soup would sometimes be served after a ball. Wine (which was comparatively weak) or perhaps beer were the drinks of choice.

Walk through the covered market to the other side and the High Street. To your left is the Abbey and Guildhall. Turn right and walk along the High Street, past the old city walls (Upper Borough Walls) into Northgate, with St. Michael's Church in front of you. Turn left up Broad Street.

STOP 6 ❦ NO. 1 THE PARAGON

We know that Mrs. Perrot will want to get us into Axford Buildings, but we all unite in particular dislike of that part of the town, and therefore hope to escape. (January 3, 1801)

O NE OF THE ATTRACTIONS OF LIVING IN BATH FOR MRS. AUSTEN WAS THE PROXIMITY TO HER BROTHER, JAMES LEIGH-PERROT, TO WHOM SHE WAS VERY CLOSE, AND HIS WIFE, JANE, WITH whom she enjoyed comparing notes on her various ailments. The Austens' eldest son, James, had been chosen to inherit the Leigh-Perrots' estate, and he would later alter his name to incorporate theirs, becoming known as James Austen-Leigh. Having lived in Bath for the winter season for many years (the rest of the year was spent at Scarlets, their country house), the Leigh-Perrots helped the Austens settle in during 1801 and introduced them to their many friends. Mrs. Austen was a regular visitor at their home, usually accompanied by one of her daughters. The fifteen-minute walk would take them along Great Pulteney Street, over the bridge, past the market, before the slow climb up Broad Street.

Walking up the hill towards the upper town, Jane would finally reach York House (now the Royal York Hotel), one of the main drop-off points for the coaches arriving from London and Basingstoke to the east. Visitors often spent their first night here recovering from the gruelling journey, then set off the next morning to find lodgings. At the back of the hotel you can still see the row of stables for the coach horses. Over the road

Axford and Paragon Buildings, 1806

on the right was the long, winding terrace of the Paragon, built in 1768–1775, and the front door of the Leigh-Perrot home at No. 1.

Further along from the Leigh-Perrots, past the Star Inn (licensed in 1760 and still open today as a public house) was St. Swithin's Church, Walcot, at the intersection of Walcot Street and Axford Buildings. The Austens had a great attachment to this church, as it had been Mr. Austen's first curacy, and he was serving there when he met Mrs. Austen. Enlarged in 1788 to include an elegant new octagonal spire, it is Bath's only remaining classical-style parish church. It was popular with the gentry for weddings; Mr. and Mrs. Austen were married here in 1764. Jane's father was later buried here.

Jane would walk back home along Walcot Street, with its institutions for the poor, a penitentiary for women, lodgings, meat markets, and food shops—a world away from the Royal Crescent and Circus. Although the Paragon and Walcot Street ran parallel, the Paragon was perched high on a cliff edge; a steep path ran between the two streets through an archway near the Leigh-Perrot's house.

Unlike the Austens, the Leigh-Perrots were wealthy and well connected. Their house was a popular venue for many small private card parties of the sort Jane detested. Bath's card parties were notorious. Wentworth suggests that Anne has "not been long enough in Bath to enjoy the card parties of the place." But Anne, like Jane, is "no card player." These tedious, pretentious evenings put a particular strain on Jane's self-control. Only a few weeks after moving to Bath she sent off a stream of complaints: "I hate tiny parties, they force one into constant exertion," "I cannot anyhow continue to find people agreeable," and "Another stupid party last night."

Although fond of her kindly uncle, Jane disliked her aunt, and her letters are full of comments about Mrs. Perrot's complaining, hypochondria, and attempts to manipulate others. A miniature of Jane Leigh-Perrot shows a formidable, somewhat joyless woman, and, for Jane at least, she was to be forever associated with her unwelcome move to Bath.

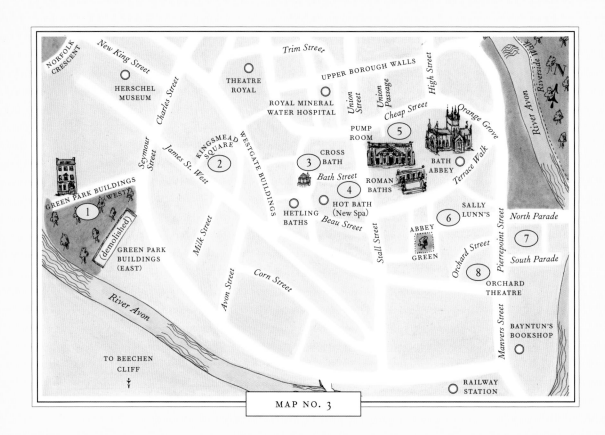

MAP NO. 3

WALK 3

Writing Again: Bath's Entertainments and the Lower Town

STOPS

Inside of Queen's Bath, 1804

WRITING AGAIN: BATH'S ENTERTAINMENTS AND THE LOWER TOWN

Her face was rather round than long—she had a bright, but not a pink colour—a clear brown complexion and very good hazle eyes—She was not, I believe, an absolute beauty, but before she left Steventon she was established as a very pretty girl, in the opinion of most of her neighbours...Her hair, a darkish brown, curled naturally—it was in short curls around her face.

IN THE SPRING OF 1803 JANE WAS TWENTY-SEVEN YEARS OLD. IT HAD BEEN TWO YEARS SINCE SHE HAD WRITTEN SERIOUSLY, AND SHE WAS NOW WELL PAST THE USUAL MARRYING AGE. THE Harry Bigg-Wither incident was an all-too-recent memory, made worse by the fact that he had been her best prospect of marriage, and the union would have secured her future and returned her to the countryside she loved. Over the previous few years she had made the best of living in the rather shallow, transient society of Bath and had developed a small circle of new friends who shared her interests. May 1803 saw Britain and France at war once again. The Austen family worried about Jane's brothers, Frank and Charles, who were back on duty. Those living in the safety of Bath followed the progress of the wars in the local newspapers.

Jane's increasing familiarity with the subtle detail of life in the city prompted her to return to what was to become her first Bath novel, *Northanger Abbey*. She took the four-year-old manuscript out of her desk drawer and revised it with a view to publication. The handwritten pages of *Northanger Abbey* had nearly been lost for good in 1798, when Jane's desk had been mistakenly put on a coach whose contents were bound for the West Indies. This mahogany writing desk was her most precious possession: "In my writing box was all my worldly wealth." With the increase in letter writing, these small, portable desks grew in popularity during the late eighteenth century and were available in the luxury shops of Bath. Their hinged, sloping lids were often lined with richly coloured velvet covering a space for writing paper, quills, seals and wax, and personal possessions.

Encouraged by Cassandra and her brother Henry, Jane moved her desk about the house in search of peace and quiet, and within a few months she had the manuscript ready to show a publisher. Henry's lawyer handled the sale to a London publisher, Crosby, who offered ten pounds for the copyright (a popular contemporary of Jane's, Maria Edgeworth, received three hundred pounds for *Belinda*) and promised swift publication.

With a novel sold and confidence restored, that winter Jane started to think about a new novel about a country family, *The Watsons*; it was to be the only new piece of writing she started in Bath. Rather than set it in the city, Jane chose instead to focus on the country society she had left behind. Sitting at her desk in Sydney Place, she picked up her quill, dipped it into ink, and started to write in her spidery, careful hand:

You know we must marry. I could do very well single for my own part; a little company, and a pleasant ball now and then, would be enough for me, if one could be young forever; but my father cannot provide for us, and it is very bad to grow old and be poor and laughed at.

The story charts Emma Watson's route to marriage, which was filled with rich but unappealing suitors and treacherous sisters such as Penelope, who "has no faith, no honour, no scruples." After the relatively optimistic novels of her earlier years, *The Watsons* is a grimly realistic portrait of unmarried women living in a country rectory with their widowed, invalid father. Miss Watson is trapped at home caring for her father while her younger sisters try to find husbands. The family has so little income that they can hardly meet the basic standards of gentility, and they dread the exposure of unexpected visits from acquaintances, especially during mealtimes. Jane talked to Cassandra at length about the plot and characters.

The Watsons provided a focus for Jane. She continued to write and was encouraged by the advertisement announcing the imminent publication of her first book. But in March 1804, after years of hypochondria, there was genuine concern for Mrs. Austen's life. Jane had to stop writing because the care of her mother, now in her sixties, would be a full-time occupation until her recovery months later.

Jane enjoyed a sociable summer holiday at Lyme Regis on the south coast in Dorset (a location later immortalised in *Persuasion*) in September 1804. She knew that, on their return, they would face the tiresome task of moving house again, for the lease was up on Sydney Place. Their aunt had told them that the new inhabitants of 4 Sydney Place had already put up their nameplate at the front door. The Austens decided to move to Green Park Buildings on the far southwestern side of the city, a group of houses they had looked at when house hunting for the first time in 1801.

STOP 1 ❧ 3 GREEN PARK BUILDINGS EAST

When my uncle went to take his second glass of water I walked with him, and in our morning's circuit we looked at two houses in Green Park Buildings, one of which pleased me very well. We walked all over it except into the garret; the dining-room is of a comfortable size, just as large as you like to fancy it; the second room about 14 ft. square. The apartment over the drawing-room pleased me particularly, because it is divided into two, the smaller one a very nice-sized dressing-room, which upon occasion might admit a bed. The aspect is south-east. The only doubt is about the dampness of the offices, of which there were symptoms. (May 5, 1801)

THE AUSTENS MOVED TO A SPACIOUS, GRAND-LOOKING HOUSE IN GREEN PARK BUILDINGS BUILT BY JOHN PALMER IN THE 1790S, WITH LATE-GEORGIAN FEATURES OF IRON BALCONIES, attractive fanlights above wide front doors, and tall slim windows. Green Park Buildings comprised two terraces, east and west, positioned around a wedge-shaped green known as Kingsmead Fields (the eastern side was bombed in World War II and no longer exists) near the banks of the River Avon. Jane was pleased that they had managed to retain a rural aspect, which compensated for the rather less glamorous route to the Pump Room through the lower town, near the slums of Avon Street. The area offered the hard-up gentry a peaceful, respectable existence at a moderate cost. Many houses were cheap at £90 per annum; similar-sized houses on the more central Gay Street cost around £150, but for that you could avoid the smell of sewage from the river in the summer.

Walk west from Green Park, where you can see the extant part of the group of houses that Jane once lived in, along Seymour Street. Turn right into James Street West (this area was heavily bombed and now is full of rather unremarkable buildings). Walking along here you will be skirting what was one of the worst areas of Bath, including Milk Street and Avon Street. Turn into Trinity Street and walk towards Kingsmead Square (c. 1730). Cross the square to Westgate Buildings on the left (where Wedgwood once had a showroom) and walk past the old St. John's Hospital (John Wood the Elder, 1728) towards Hot Bath Street.

STOP 2 ❧ KINGSMEAD SQUARE AND THE LOWER TOWN

Prettier musings of high-wrought love and eternal constancy, could never have passed along the streets of Bath, than Anne was sporting from Camden-place to Westgate-buildings. It was almost enough to spread purification and perfume all the way. (Persuasion)

I T WAS COMMON KNOWLEDGE THAT BATH HAD TWO VERY DIFFERENT FACES. WITH DAMP HOVELS HUGGING THE BANKS OF THE NOXIOUS RIVER AVON, THE LOWER TOWN WAS A FAR CRY from the wealth and cleanliness of the Upper Town. The Lower Town was a world of plague, beggars, and petty crime. The gutters were full of dead animals and excrement, and those from the Upper Town who ventured there complained about the vile smells. Most visitors travelling between the Baths and Pump Room skirted the lower side of town.

Anyone taking a wrong turn could end up at Westgate Buildings. Back in 1798–1799, when writing *Northanger Abbey*, Jane would have had little, if any, knowledge of the Lower Town. But by the time she wrote *Persuasion* she had a resident's understanding of the city and could give a fuller picture of Bath. Ignoring social convention and her father's wishes, Anne Elliot visits an old Bath schoolfriend who has fallen on hard times and is reduced to living in Westgate Buildings, a place so foul that only Anne in her enraptured state could walk through and remain oblivious to the squalor. Nearby Corn Street, known as Little 'Ell by the locals, was reckoned to be the worst street; its crowded slums offered shared rooms with flea-ridden beds at threepence a night for the thousands of poorly paid craftsmen who made the trinkets for the luxury shops, along with the tradesmen, servants, and coachmen who flocked to Bath. Beer and gin flowed freely in the area's many taverns. Avon Street, where prostitutes plied their trade, was the centre of the slum. This area also provided large storerooms for the elegant furniture awaiting the orders of decorators charged with fitting up a whole rented house in just three days for clients waiting at a local hotel.

Walk along Hot Bath Street past the Hetling Pump Room and the Hot Bath to the Cross Bath, the location of the new Spa.

Cross Bath, Bath Street, 1804

STOP 3 ❧ CROSS BATH AND THE SPA

What must I tell you of Edward?…He drinks at the Hetling Pump, is to bathe to-morrow, and try
electricity on Tuesday. He proposed the latter himself to Dr. Fellowes, who made no objection to it,
but I fancy we are all unanimous in expecting no advantage from it. (June 2, 1799)

THE SMALL, DECORATIVE LIMESTONE BUILDINGS OF THE CROSS BATH (REMODELLED IN 1798 WITH AN ADAM-INSPIRED FAÇADE) AND THE HETLING PUMP, TOGETHER WITH THE HOT Bath and the surrounding quiet, cobbled streets remain just as Jane knew them two hundred years ago. In her day the streets would have been full of sedan chairs bearing the infirm, jostling to get to and from the entrances of the Baths.

The Baths were the historic reason for the city's development, but the spa water was at the centre of much controversy. It was debated whether it was the temperature, method of application, mineral content, or presence of sulphur that gave it its healing power. Cold water was considered an ideal cure for swollen joints and ulcers; warm water was said to relieve asthma, hysterical disorders, and circulation problems, and to act as a general detoxifier. The most common diagnoses in the Bath General Hospital's admission books during this period were arthritis, paralysis (palsy), and various skin diseases.

With death and disease such a prominent feature of life in Georgian England, the slightest cough or stomachache would make the sufferer nervous about the cause and possible outcome. Widespread hypochondria amongst both men and women was the inevitable result. The opportunity to go to Bath was seized upon by bored country wives and daughters at the slightest hint of a symptom in themselves or their relatives. With little to offer in terms of real cures, the many doctors who had been attracted to Bath made their fortune with diagnoses and prescriptions of hot- or cold-water treatments and dubious pills and potions.

Having put up with her mother's constant complaints about her health, Jane was intolerant of hypochondria. Her portrayal of the lazy hypochondriac Mary Musgrove, in *Persuasion*, makes clear her disapproval. Reflecting the preoccupations of life at the time, Jane makes many allusions to illness and fatal diseases in her novels. Doctors are always in attendance, prescribing potions or bleeding the patient, but strength of will appears to be the main route to recovery for the sick.

The many different baths in the city were designed for specific purposes and clienteles. The Cross Bath, which attracted celebrities, had a spectators' gallery. There was even a special bath at the southern entrance to the city to clean the mud-spattered horses with water drained from the King's Bath. This ancient spring pumped out more than 180,000 gallons of water a day at a constant temperature of 116 degrees Fahrenheit. The King's Bath was adjacent to the Pump Room and next to the new women-only Queen's Bath (this was removed in the late nineteenth century, but the separate entrances can still be seen from Stall Street). These open-air stone baths, despite being surrounded by columns and statues, were as far from the Assembly Rooms as you could imagine. The usual social rules of separation of the sexes did not apply here, and the sick mixed with the healthy in a malodorous stew. Every day the water was revived with a sprinkling of herbs to obscure the unpleasant smells. Male and female bathers had to wear drab brown canvas tunics, leaving only elaborate headgear as the means to signify one's status.

❖

Everywhere, day and night you would see the traditional sedans swarming around the city streets. After dark a travelling sedan had to carry a lighted lamp or be accompanied by a link boy holding a flambeau. (Tobias Smollett, The Expedition of Humphry Clinker, *1771)*

The black-painted leather sedan chair, an enclosed chair carried on poles by two men, was an early forerunner of the taxi. By 1740 they were common sights in the cities of Europe, and in some places they remained in use into the twentieth century. As Bath expanded, the number of sedans grew from around sixty in 1745 to two hundred and fifty in 1793–1794. By this time they were regulated, and each chair had a large white licence number painted on the side. The sedan chairmen carried sick or elderly tourists from their bedsides, already in their bathing costumes, to the waiting chair, and then down the slopes from their lodgings to take a cure in one of the baths. Many visitors used sedan chairs for their daily round, and the chairs were especially in demand at night after concerts or balls at the Assembly Rooms or theatre. Privately owned chairs had richly upholstered interiors and a variety of decorative features, from patterned doors to gilded coronets on the roofs. (Examples of public and private sedans can be seen in the Pump Room.)

A Modern Belle going to the Rooms at Bath, 1796. Contemporary caricature of Bath life, showing a sedan chair accomodating fashion-conscious visitors.

Bath's Local Improvement Act of 1793 restricted sedan service to twenty-two listed waiting areas across the city. Four chairs were allowed on South Parade, eight in the Abbey Churchyard (of which there could be no more than four outside the Pump Room), six by the Cross Bath, six in both Queen Square and the Circus, four in St. James's Square, six in Lansdown Crescent, and eight in Laura Place.

Bath was known to be a wet city; in *Persuasion*, Wentworth's first purchase on arriving is an umbrella. Smollett's Humphry Clinker condemned the practice of leaving sedans out in the rain: "The chairs stand soaking in the open street, from morning to night, till they become so many boxes of wet leather." Chairmen tucked their double-milled waterproof greatcoats behind them to prevent splashing. Rheumatism was an occupational hazard. The expansion of the city up the steep northern slopes such as Lansdown took its toll on chairmen's health, and at one point they went on strike for a day until a higher fare was granted for uphill journeys.

Walk along Bath Street towards Stall Street and the Pump Room.

STOP 4 ❧ BATH STREET

Edward has been pretty well for this last week, and as the waters have never disagreed with him in any respect, we are inclined to hope that he will derive advantage from them in the end. Everybody encourages us in this expectation, for they all say that the effect of the waters cannot be negative, and many are the instances in which their benefit is felt afterwards more than on the spot. (June 11, 1799)

FOR MANY YEARS, THE AREA AROUND THE BATHS REMAINED LARGELY AS IT HAD BEEN IN THE MEDIEVAL PERIOD. BUT IN THE EARLY 1790S THE BATH CORPORATION DECIDED TO CREATE an elegant and convenient route between the Cross Bath, popular with the aristocracy and royalty, and a new Pump Room.

Many older buildings were pulled down, clearing the way for the new Bath Street. Faced with the challenge of matching the grandeur of Wood's Upper Town in a constricted space, Thomas Baldwin, then the city's chief surveyor, came up with an ingenious plan. He used perspective theory in the form of an unusually low roofline to suggest a long, wide street on his redesigned Cross Bath. He added fashionable Adam flourishes and a colonnade on both sides of the street so that pedestrians could enjoy a clean, sheltered walk.

This was a regular route into town for Jane, and walking under the colonnade of Bath Street past Elizabeth Gregory's haberdashery, it would have been impossible to forget the dreadful scandal of August 1799 involving her family. Jane Leigh-Perrot had been at the haberdasher's shop, where some black lace had been added to her parcel of new trimmings. As she walked across the Church Yard in front of the Abbey and Pump Room she was accosted by the owners and accused of stealing. The victim of a con, she denied the charges furiously but was nevertheless sent to Taunton Jail, some sixty miles south of Bath, where she spent many miserable months facing the prospect of deportation to Australia. The *Bath Chronicle* published a long account of the trial in spring 1800. Mrs. Leigh-Perrot was eventually proved innocent.

Cross Stall Street and walk under the colonnade into the Abbey Church Yard to the northern side of the Pump Room. The entrance here takes you into the tearooms and spa water pump, as well as the Roman Baths.

The Pump Room, 1806

STOP 5 ❧ THE PUMP ROOM

As soon as the divine service was over, the Thorpes and the Allens eagerly joined each other; and after staying long enough in the Pump-room to discover that the crowd was insupportable, and that there was not a genteel face to be seen, which everybody discovers every Sunday throughout the season, they hastened away to the Crescent, to breathe the fresh air of better company. (Northanger Abbey)

AN INTEGRAL PART OF THE BATH CURE WAS TO DRINK THE WATER AT THE PUMP ROOMS, WHERE THE WOMAN IN CHARGE OF THE PUMP DISPENSED REGULAR DOSES OR GLASSES OF SPA WATER to subscribing customers. "Mr. Allen after drinking his glass of water, joined some gentlemen to talk over the politics of the day and compare the accounts of the newspapers" (*Northanger Abbey*). Water mains did not exist then, but Bath was advanced in comparison with the rest of England. It had a fledgling water supply service provided by private companies who piped clean water from the hill springs of Lansdown into well-off households. Others had to send servants out to collect water from the surface wells in the street.

Opened 1795, the generously proportioned, sophisticated Pump Room replaced the original John Harvey rooms of 1706 to cater to the large numbers of increasingly demanding visitors. An impressive stone colonnade was designed to screen the Abbey Yard and Pump Room from busy Stall Street. The public rooms were made of Bath stone with tall arched windows along one side and an elegant entranceway facing a large open paved area outside. These public rooms consisted of a large ballroom and many other rooms for gatherings and concerts.

In 1730, while digging sewage trenches, builders discovered a gilded bronze head from an ancient statue of the Roman goddess Minerva. Sixty years later, while laying foundations for the new Pump Room, a solid Roman pavement was unearthed four metres below ground, revealing Bath's great Roman temple. (Nearly a century later, in the 1880s, the true extent of the two-thousand-year-old Roman Baths was revealed by Victorian architects to great public excitement.)

By Jane's time the Pump Room had become the social centre of the city and the main place for visitors to meet and look over the new arrivals in town. Jane frequently alluded to the intense embarrassment caused by any contravention of the social rules of the time, and the Elliots of *Persuasion* offer much scope for incident: "The Bath paper one morning announced the arrival of the Dowager Viscountess Dalrymple," a cousin of the Elliots but also a member of the nobility and therefore of higher rank than Sir Walter, for whom "the agony was, how to introduce themselves properly." Distinctions would not only be made between members of a family but also between country and city society: "While the Musgroves were of the first society in the country" they would not move in similar circles in the city and might even be snubbed. Sir Walter was also faced with the difficult task of reconciling an embarrassing financial situation with acquaintances of different social classes:

"I suspect," said Sir Walter coolly, "that Admiral Croft will be best known in Bath as the renter of Kellynch-Hall. Elizabeth, may we venture to present him and his wife in Laura Place?" "Oh! no, I think not. Situated

as we are with Lady Dalrymple, cousins, we ought to be very careful not to embarrass her with acquaintance she might not approve…We had better leave the Crofts to find their own level."

The Elliots' careful choice of address had been worth the effort: "Their acquaintance was exceedingly sought after…[They] were perpetually having cards left by people of whom they knew nothing." Their address would have been found in the publicly available visitor's book in the Pump Room, as could the Tilneys':

Catherine…was more impatient than ever to be at the Pump-room, that she might inform herself of General Tilney's lodgings, for though she believed they were in Milsom-street, she was not certain of the house…To Milsom-street she was directed; and having made herself perfect in the number, hastened away with eager steps and a beating heart to pay her visit, explain her conduct, and be forgiven; tripping lightly though the church-yard. (Northanger Abbey)

Walk from the Abbey Churchyard to the front of the western façade of the Abbey—previously a Roman temple, Saxon Church, and Norman cathedral—which has an impressive fan vaulted ceiling. Walk along Abbey Street into Abbey Green, built by John Wood the Elder in 1727, and then across to North Parade Passage to the east.

Bath Abbey and the Orange Grove, 1805

STOP 6 ❧ SALLY LUNN'S BAKERY AND CAFÉ

AFTER LEAVING THE PUMP ROOM, JANE COULD BROWSE IN THE BOOKSHOPS AND WALK ALONG THE NARROW STREET CALLED NORTH PARADE PASSAGE TO THE RENOWNED SALLY LUNN'S bakery at no. 4. Built in 1622, this is one of the oldest houses in Bath. Now a café with a small museum, it was the home of the large, slightly sweet, brioche-style Bath buns that Jane enjoyed. Back in 1801 she had written to Cassandra about "disordering [her] stomach with bath bunns." An advertisement of 1799 from W. Dalmer's bakery on Walcot Street offered a warm breakfast delivered to your door: "Sally Luns and other breakfast cakes sent out warm every morning in a portable oven." It went on to instruct visitors in the correct way to eat the famous local delicacy: "They should be cut in half and have melted butter poured over them and left to soak in before eating."

The streets to the east of the abbey through the passage and around the Terrace Walk and Orange Grove had been the most fashionable area of the city in the mid-eighteenth century. Terrace Walk had been home to many luxury shops and the old Parade Coffee House, one of the first of many coffeehouses in Bath. The only extant eighteenth-century shopfront is at No. 1, with a façade of Ionic columns, arches, and leaf carvings.

Continue along North Parade Passage and, with Terrace Walk to your left, cross Pierrepoint Street to North Parade. Walk along North Parade's broad pavements until you reach Duke Street on the right, where the once grand and glamorous houses are now in a dreadful state of repair. Turn left onto South Parade and walk towards the river.

STOP 7 ❧ NORTH AND SOUTH PARADES

THESE TALL TERRACES WITH THEIR BROAD, LEVEL PAVEMENTS ADJACENT TO THE RIVER AVON WERE BUILT IN THE 1740S. THEY WERE THE SECOND PHASE OF JOHN WOOD THE ELDER'S grand plan to provide accommodation near the entertainments of the Lower Assembly Rooms (1709) and the famous Orchard Theatre. Later, as the town developed to the north, a second Assembly Rooms was built (the Upper Rooms), leading to intense rivalry. The timetables for balls and concerts had to be carefully planned to minimise schedule clashes and to ensure that entertainments were available every night of the week.

In a town known as much for its oppressive summer heat as its rain, the North Parade had been created specifically to offer the respite of a shaded promenade. By the early nineteenth century the area had become markedly less popular because of competition from nearby Great Pulteney Street and from the Upper Rooms. The corporation tried to combat this by improving access from the Pump Room, building the wider York Street in 1805.

By autumn 1804 Jane was benefiting from the quiet seclusion of their house at Green Park. She was busy writing *The Watsons* but had increasing concerns about the delayed publication of *Northanger Abbey*, which had yet to appear despite being advertised the year before.

December 1804 was blighted by Mr. Austen's persistent ill health; he was increasingly weak and now used a walking stick. Jane's birthday was marred by the sudden death of her Hampshire friend and mentor, Madame

North Parade, 1804

Lefroy, who had been thrown from her horse. Jane's response to crisis was often to embark on long walks. The North and South Parades, on the opposite side of the city, were among her favourite destinations.

The Parades area enjoyed only a brief period of glamour, and today, after much postwar building, the area is rather shabby, a far cry from the perfectly preserved Upper Town. It is, however, worth venturing along Manvers Street (the continuation southwards of Pierrepoint Street) towards the railway station (1841) to the nineteenth-century Bayntun's Bookbinder and Antiquarian Book and Print Shop still housed in its original building on Manvers Street. In addition to a fascinating stock of antiquarian books and prints, there is also a book museum containing, among other things, a collection of early editions of Jane Austen's novels, as well as prints of the city of Bath during the time she lived there.

Walk along South Parade, turning right into Pierrepoint Street (Horatio Nelson stayed at No. 2 in 1781). Cross the road, pass under the colonnaded entrance to cobbled Pierrepoint Place, and round the corner into Orchard Street and the old Theatre Royal.

STOP 8 ❧ THE THEATRE ROYAL

Here are a variety of amusements, I really believe I shall always be talking of Bath. (Northanger Abbey)

J ANE LOVED THE THEATRE, WHETHER LIVELY HOME THEATRICALS WITH HER BROTHERS OR NIECES, OR GRAND PERFORMANCES IN BATH OR LONDON. THE HIGH-QUALITY ORCHARD STREET theatre that opened in 1750 was a major attraction of Bath for her, and with three performances three times a week, there were plenty of plays to choose from. The theatre employed one of the most imaginative set designers in the country, Thomas French. It was the only theatre outside London to be granted (in 1768) a prestigious royal patent entitling it be called "Royal."

The Bath theatrical evenings Jane attended would usually combine a main play with song and dance interludes and a comic piece to finish. Modern comedies of manners and melodrama were also popular. The emotionally charged performances of the famous actress Sarah Siddons captivated audiences between 1778 and 1792. Although Siddons was finally lured to the London stage, crowds would line the streets for her occasional guest performances back in Bath.

The theatre in Orchard Street was chosen as the location for an important scene in *Northanger Abbey*:

No Tilneys appeared to plague or please her; she feared that, among the many perfections of the family a

fondness for plays was not to be ranked… The comedy so well suspended her care, that no one, observing her
during the first four acts, would have supposed she had any wretchedness about her. On the beginning of
the fifth, however, the sudden view of Mr. Henry Tilney and his father joining a party in the opposite box,
recalled her to anxiety and distress.

Jane describes the typical box-hopping behaviour of the audience, and it is here that John Thorpe suggests to the greedy General Tilney that Catherine is an heiress.

By 1805, with demand for tickets outstripping capacity, the theatre moved to larger premises at Sawclose between Queen Square and Westgate Buildings. (It was here that Charles Musgrove, in the closing chapters of *Persuasion*, reserved a box big enough for a party of nine.)

✦

On Monday morning, January 21, 1805, Jane's beloved father died after a sudden and violent forty-eight-hour illness. Cassandra was away helping her friend Martha nurse her dying mother, leaving Jane alone to support her mother and write the difficult letters to her brothers telling them that "our dear father has closed his virtuous and happy life."

Jane was pragmatic in her thankfulness that he and they were spared a protracted illness, and her behaviour at this time was guided by a sense of duty and propriety. The funeral was held that Saturday at St. Swithin's Church, Walcot, after which the long mourning period began. Jane, Cassandra, and Mrs. Austen assembled

Letter from Jane Austen to her brother, Frank, January 29, 1805 mourning clothes, and mourning brooches were made up.

The rules and rituals of mourning make many appearances in Jane's novels. *Persuasion* opens with the Elliots in mourning for Mr. William Elliot's wife, and Elizabeth grudgingly makes the minimum gesture by wearing black ribbons. Those closest to the deceased, including a family's servants, were obliged to wear full mourning, but black lace, veils, and ribbons could be worn by others wishing to make a gesture.

On a practical level, too, Mr. Austen's death was disastrous news for Jane, Cassandra, and their mother. The clergy pension of six hundred pounds would cease, leaving them effectively penniless. Unable to earn an income to retain their social position, and with little money of their own, their welfare became the responsibility of Jane's brothers. Accommodation was a key part of retaining a veneer of respectability, and it would take up a large proportion of what little income they had. They decided to spend the summers with Henry or Edward and the season in Bath, where Mrs. Austen could be near her doctor and have the company of her brother and sister-in-law. The sisters had always been good at keeping their accounts, but now a great deal of their time would be spent organizing what little money they had and finding somewhere smaller and cheaper to live. They would move twice during the next year to ever smaller and less salubrious accommodations.

As Mrs. Austen joined the ranks of widows who frequented the public and private rooms of Bath, her unmarried, bereaved daughters would become objects of pity. Jane's experiences of loss during this time informed much of her later Bath novel, *Persuasion*, which includes a high number of widowed characters, male and female. But for now, her recently revived interest in writing was halted by this change in circumstances.

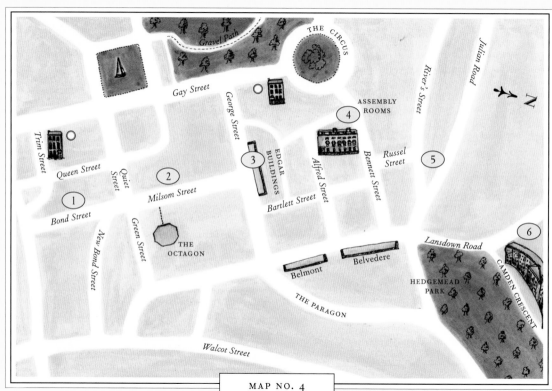

THE CIRCUS

Gravel Path

Gay Street

George Street

Trim Street

Queen Street

Quiet Street

Milsom Street

Bond Street

New Bond Street

Green Street

THE OCTAGON

EDGAR BUILDINGS

Bartlett Street

ASSEMBLY ROOMS

Alfred Street

Bennett Street

Russel Street

River's Street

Julian Road

N

Belmont

Belvedere

THE PARAGON

Lansdown Road

HEDGEMEAD PARK

CAMDEN CRESCENT

Walcot Street

1

2

3

4

5

6

MAP NO. 4

WALK 4

Shopping, Fashion, and Dancing: Bond Street and Milsom Street to Camden Crescent

Portrait believed to be of Jane Austen as a young girl, c. 1792-3

SHOPPING, FASHION, AND DANCING: BOND STREET AND MILSOM STREET TO CAMDEN CRESCENT

What a different set are we now moving in! But seven years I suppose are enough to change every pore of one's skin, & every feeling of one's mind. (April 8, 1805)

SINCE HER FIRST VISIT TO BATH SEVEN YEARS BEFORE IN 1797, JANE'S LIFE HAD BEEN DRAMATICALLY ALTERED: YOUTHFUL AMBITIONS FOR HER WRITING HAD BEEN DASHED, AND HOPES for love and romance had come to nothing. And now she was effectively impoverished in a city where appearances were everything. The mature, melancholy tone of *Persuasion* could well have its origins in the harsh realities faced by Jane in those last months in Bath.

When writing to her brother Frank immediately after Mr. Austen's death in January 1805, Jane had thought that they might be moving back to Steventon once the remaining three months of their lease at Green Park Buildings were up. But Mrs. Austen chose to stay in Bath, and by April they had left their large, comfortable house and moved back into the centre of town to a more affordable and convenient accommodation at 25 Gay Street.

Mr. Austen's sudden death had left Mrs. Austen and her two daughters at the mercy of relatives. Each brother contributed £50 a year, and Edward was able to afford somewhat more. Cassandra's inheritance of £1000 from the estate of her fiancé, Thomas Fowle, gave her a small annual income, and Mrs. Austen also had a small inheritance. Only Jane had nothing to contribute to the household budget—the £10 from the sale of *Northanger Abbey* had long since been spent. In the end they managed to scrape together a total income of £450 a year—enough to keep a couple of servants, eat relatively well, and have a small amount of spending money. An acceptable address was more important than space, so they economised on accommodation, by far the largest expense. Although they had previously considered Gay Street too expensive, they felt they could afford a small group of rooms—much like the rooms rented by Admiral and Mrs. Croft in *Persuasion*. The following year the Austens were to make one final move in Bath to the backwater of Trim Street (west of Bond Street), which they had avoided in the past on account of Cassandra's inexplicable dread of it.

Jane and Cassandra were resourceful and had always taken money seriously; their aim was to minimise the impact of a smaller income on their lifestyle, and not be reduced to wearing cast-offs and surviving on traditional pease soup of vegetables and dried peas. They all knew that plans would have to be made for the future. With Cassandra away in Hampshire for much of the spring, the entertainment of Mrs. Austen and the organisation of the household fell to Jane, leaving no time for *The Watsons*.

This walk follows Anne Elliot's footsteps through Bath along the long, slow climb from Mollands at the lower western end of Milsom Street (now occupied by a shop) to her new home at Camden-place (now Camden Crescent) in the upper town. The path from the medieval heart of the city into the commercial Georgian area and through the small streets towards the Assembly Rooms and the residential streets around it was a well-worn route for tourists and residents alike.

STOP 1 ❧ BOND STREET

Our heroine's entrée into life could not take place till after three or four days had been spent in learning what was mostly worn ... When all these matters were arranged, the important evening came which was to usher her into the Upper Rooms. (Northanger Abbey)

BOND STREET, MILSOM STREET, AND THE MANY EXCLUSIVE STREETS RADIATING FROM THEM FORMED THE LUXURY SHOPPING QUARTER OF BATH, WHICH WAS ONE OF THE MAIN ATTRACtions for visitors. Bath was famous for offering an unrivalled assortment of high-quality shops within a compact area noted for its wide, clean pavements. An enormous range of goods was on offer: fabrics, exotic foods, popular prints, jewellery, confectionery, flowers, books, hats, furnishings, decorated china, medicines, portraits, beauty products, and art materials. Pyramids of exotic pineapples and figs were stacked in the windows of fruit shops, and delicious ices were for sale in confectioners. The shops on Bond Street were every bit as luxurious as those on London's Bond Street. Cities such as London and Bath, with their enticing shop-front window displays, were showcases for Britain's newly developed manufacturing skills. In *Sense and Sensibility*, Charlotte Palmer's "eye was caught by every thing pretty, expensive, or new."

Being on constant display in Bath was a change for countrywomen used to dressing up only occasionally.

Visitors and residents changed outfits many times a day, and Jane saw a great variety of elaborate dress. Jane decided that she urgently needed new dresses, as she felt "tired & ashamed" of her old ones: "I even blush at the sight of the wardrobe which contains them." She was adept at spotting the turn of a cuff, types of ribbon pleating, and bonnet decoration. Her letters are full of these details.

Even before moving to Bath she had planned her first purchases, telling Cassandra:

I shall want two new coloured gowns for the summer, for my pink one will not do more than clear me from Steventon. I shall not trouble you, however, to get more than one of them, and that is to be a plain brown cambric muslin, for morning wear; the other, which is to be a very pretty yellow and white cloud, I mean to buy in Bath. Buy two brown ones, if you please, and both of a length, but one longer than the other—it is for a tall woman. Seven yards for my mother, seven yards and a half for me; a dark brown, but the kind of brown is left to your own choice, and I had rather they were different, as it will be always something to say, to dispute about which is the prettiest. They must be cambric muslin." (January 25, 1801)

The simple white muslin dress was the fashion sensation of the early 1800s, and Jane loved the style. "I mean to have my new white one made up now, in case we should go to the Rooms again next Monday," she wrote in 1801. *Mansfield Park*'s Edmund Bertram claims that "a woman can never be too fine while she is all in white."

Muslin was a new finely woven, light cotton fabric which was eminently flexible: it was washable, could be hand embroidered in many different ways and dyed in variety of pale colours for daytime wear. Originally from India, it soon became so popular that it was manufactured in England to keep pace with demand. Popular hand-stitched muslin decorations for eveningwear included white beads to give a subtly shimmering effect, or "spots" (knots of thread), thousands of which were needed for a single dress. One of Catherine Morland's new dresses is tamboured, meaning that is had been finely embroidered (using a wooden tambour frame to stretch the fabric) with coloured patterns of leaves and flowers using a kind of chain stitch. Taken to extremes (some women would lie in cold baths to encourage the fabric to shrink to fit), the transparency and clinging qualities of muslin were considered too revealing. The *Ladies Monthly Magazine* of March 1803 noted the trend of "high-bred young ladies who were dressed or rather undressed in all the nakedness of the mode."

Daywear involved warmer clothes than in the evenings, chosen from a variety of cloaks, large scarves, long coats called pelisses, or perhaps a full riding-habit outfit of thick fabric. In the warmer months, brightly coloured velvet, wool, or silk jackets called spencers would be worn over pretty white day dresses. These were cropped to follow the raised waistlines of dresses, had a high collar, and often were decorated with embroidery and beads. Confident upper- and middle-class girls looking for a rich husband favoured this eye-catching combination. Jane owned at least one spencer, and a few years later mentioned, "My kerseymere Spencer is quite the comfort of our even'g walks."

In the 1790s a new style of long, buttoned-up coat, called a pelisse, became popular. Pelisses were costly and were made of either a soft twilled silk called sarsenet or of velvet, and they were lined with wool and trimmed with beads, ribbons, and fur. Some, made of burnt orange sarsenet with a wafting swansdown collar dappled with black feathery tufts, were highly glamorous. Jane and Cassandra both had at least one pelisse each, and once Jane was receiving an income from her writing she bought herself a silk pelisse for special occasions. Fanny Price, of *Mansfield Park*, suffered socially as "she neither played the pianoforte nor wore fine pelisses."

Amongst the milliners, hosiers, watchmakers, wine merchants, gunsmiths, and glovers of Bond Street was Barrett's Circulating Library, one of Bath's most popular quality bookshops and the one most likely to have been regularly visited by Jane. By charging about three pence per loan item, these libraries made borrowing a cheap alternative to buying books, which were expensive. One of the Austen's favourites, *Evelina*, by Fanny Burney, cost about eight shillings for a three-volume set (sewn but without a binding). When Jane's first novel was published six years later, it cost fifteen shillings for three volumes.

Bath was unusual in having so many excellent bookshops and libraries, and this was one of the reasons for its popularity with writers. The old painted sign on the wall of what was Godwin's Circulating Library halfway along Milsom Street survives today. And there are still some wonderful original shop-fronts along Bond Street, such as No. 7 and No. 8, with bow windows and decorative mouldings.

Walk from Bond Street to the southern end of Milsom Street, exploring the many small streets radiating from this area.

STOP 2 ❧ MILSOM STREET

Walking up Milsom Street, she had the good fortune to meet with the Admiral [Croft]. He was standing by himself, at a print shop window ... 'I can never get by this shop without stopping' (Persuasion)

LIKE ADMIRAL CROFT, JANE AND CASSANDRA ENJOYED VISITING THE ART AND PRINT SHOPS OF BATH. THESE DISPLAYED ROW UPON ROW OF TINY WATERCOLOUR PANS IN MYRIAD colours sent from Soho in London, tin boxes to contain them, inks, and newly made paper from Bath's paper mills. Of particular interest to Jane were the cheap popular prints, especially those by satirical artists such as Thomas Rowlandson, artist of the *Comforts of Bath* series.

Many people collected prints, which they pasted directly onto the walls of a dedicated print room or placed in thin black wooden frames and mounted on drawing room walls. Landscape and city views were popular, especially of places such as Bath. In 1804–1805 the artist J. C. Nattes was busy in the streets and public rooms of Bath drawing his souvenir series *Images of Bath*. By 1806 these were printed and displayed in the shops.

Jane's descriptions in her letters of typical days out shopping showed how carefully such a day would be planned. Edward would often give her a gift of five pounds to spend on fabric for a new dress, shoes, or lavender scent. Catherine Morland was given ten pounds by her father for her Bath holiday and told to write for more if she needed it. Early shops would sell from a counter where the (usually male) shopkeeper would advise cus-

Milsom Street looking south towards Bond Street, 1805

tomers and fetch selected items; soon though, the new practice took hold of allowing customers view tabletop displays and pick up and examine goods themselves. Regency England turned shop display into an art form, although the original idea belonged to Josiah Wedgwood, the innovative ceramics producer.

Shopping was not then considered to be a leisure pursuit but was taken seriously. Getting the right price was considered important; Jane deliberately has John Thorpe slip up socially when he boasts of not haggling over the price of his gig, in contrast to the aristocratic Henry Tilney, who prided himself on getting the best price for fabric. People of the time frequently refer to the "business" of shopping, and Jane compared prices and quality and took her "commissions" on behalf of friends and family very seriously.

Milsom Street was full of different shops, but the only one Jane chose to describe in her novels was the fashionable sweetshop Mollands, at No. 2. It was the site, in *Persuasian*, of Anne and Wentworth's meeting in Bath, where he overheard an unfortunate conversation between Anne's companions—her sister, Elizabeth, and Mrs. Clay—about the likelihood of Mr. Elliot and Anne getting married.

Luxury shopping was not confined to the main thoroughfares; there were also adjacent small streets, such as Quiet Street and Green Street, some of which still have original cobbled roads. Green Street, made famous by its connections with Dr. William Oliver, the inventor of the Bath Oliver biscuit, was so exclusive that the corporation turned down a request from a butcher to take a shop there. Dr. Oliver bequeathed the recipe for these plain, dry digestive aids to his coachman, Atkins, who set up business at 13 Green Street and made himself a fortune. The business passed through a succession of hands, and the biscuits are still available today.

STOP 3 ❧ EDGAR BUILDINGS

IN NORTHANGER ABBEY, THE THORPES STAYED JUST YARDS AWAY FROM THE TILNEYS IN THE CHEAPER EDGAR BUILDINGS AT THE TOP OF MILSOM STREET, JUST ACROSS GEORGE street. This area was developed in rather piecemeal fashion as part of a scheme in the early 1760s to link the major north–south thoroughfares of Gay Street and Broad Street. Along the northern side of the street sit three short terraces built in the 1760s. On the western side, towards Gay Street, 3 Miles's Buildings has the original Venetian windows and Gothic-style window bars and doorways, with an original hood and mouldings. Nine imposing central houses form Edgar Buildings, an address that features prominently in *Northanger Abbey* and was home to many famous visitors and residents. To the east, Bennett Street provided another route to the Assembly Rooms.

Guidebooks of the time describe how "from the upper part of Milsom-street through Bond-street and Union Street, to the Pump-room, now constitutes the midday promenade of the fashionable visitants." And this is certainly the route most followed by *Northanger Abbey*'s Catherine and Isabella, along which the latter saw "the prettiest hat you can imagine, in a shop window in Milsom-Street just now…with coquelicot [poppy-red] ribbons instead of green: I quite longed for it."

Continue along Bartlett Street and turn left into Alfred Street and walk around to the right to the entrance of the Assembly Rooms.

Assembly Rooms, 1806

STOP 4 ❧ ASSEMBLY ROOMS

The season was full, the room crowded, and the two ladies squeezed in as well as they could…With more care for the safety of her new gown than for the comfort of her protegee, Mrs. Allen made her way through the throng of men by the door…They saw nothing of the dancers but the high feathers of some of the ladies…By a continued exertion of strength and ingenuity, they found themselves at last in the passage behind the highest bench…It was a splendid sight; and she began, for the first time that evening, to feel herself at a ball. (Northanger Abbey)

THE ASSEMBLY ROOMS WERE BUILT BY JOHN WOOD THE YOUNGER IN 1769, AT A COST OF MORE THAN TWENTY THOUSAND POUNDS, AS A PLACE FOR SOCIETY TO TAKE TEA, GOSSIP, PLAY cards, and attend concerts and balls. The rooms consisted of a one-hundred-foot-long ballroom with space along one side for invalids' sedan chairs; the relatively small card room into which Mr. Allen disappears; a long, narrow tearoom; and the Octagon Room near the entrance used as a waiting area. There were special seats for peeresses and a rule that allowed time "for ladies of precedence to take their places" between minuets and country dances.

By 1805 the Upper Rooms were open every day to both men and women for card games. Every other Sunday they were open for a promenade around the ballroom. The Upper Rooms were the main venue for public entertainments during the season, and most visitors would subscribe to the balls. There was a dress ball on Monday, card assembly on Tuesday, concert on Wednesday, fancy ball on Thursday. The *1801 Guide to Bath* described the balls: "As spectacles, they must be considered, when well attended, as the most elegant and magnificent in Europe." The balls would start at 7 PM "and conclude precisely at 11 PM even if in the middle of a dance."

> *The important evening came, which was to usher her into the upper rooms. Her hair was cut and dressed by the best hand, her clothes put on with care, and both Mrs. Allen and her maid declared she looked just as she should.*
> (Northanger Abbey)

Most towns of any size had their own assemblies, which were especially important in rural areas as a meeting place. Jane particularly enjoyed the lively country dances popular at the time, and she attended many balls at Assembly Rooms and private houses. By the time she arrived in Bath at the season's end in 1801, she was disappointed by the scant assemblies on offer. There were no crowds to squeeze through as there had been in the Bath of *Northanger Abbey*, when more than one thousand people could fill the Rooms. This novel reflects Jane's earliest experiences of Bath and is full of excitement—and of confusion over the right way to behave. Catherine feels disappointed by the ball and by Mrs. Allen, who "took more care for the safety of her gown than the safety of her protégée," and she was embarrassed at their knowing no one and being unable to dance or take tea in the usual manner. The narrator in *Northanger Abbey* is amused that Mrs. Morland's only worries for her daughter attending her first ball concerned her catching cold, as she was blissfully unaware of the possibilities of far greater dangers to her daughter's reputation and future.

In contrast to *Northanger Abbey*'s depiction of a hectic evening out in Bath, Anne Elliot's unnerving experience in the Upper Rooms in *Persuasion*—where two men unexpectedly vie for her attention—is that of a more experienced woman. While Catherine lies awake agonising over "what gown and what head-dress she should wear" to her first ball, "debating between her spotted and her tamboured muslin," Anne has more serious things on her mind.

These very different experiences of Bath's assemblies are set more than a decade apart and indicate the shift in the city's fortunes from a fashionable centre of society to the city of choice for retirees and hard-up gentry. The relatively empty, sedate Upper Rooms of *Persuasion*, set in 1814, are a mere shadow of their heyday, the late eighteenth-century setting of *Northanger Abbey*.

The site is now the Assembly Rooms and Museum of Costume (see p. 129). You can walk around the rooms just as Jane did—into the Ballroom, the Octagon Room, and the Tea Room. The Assembly Rooms Tea Room serves delicious teas and is open throughout the day. The museum downstairs houses a fascinating collection of historic clothes and accessories with a well-stocked bookshop.

From the Assembly Rooms, walk onto Bennett Street alongside the northern side of the rooms, and then left onto Russel Street, where you can still see Georgian torch snuffers and boot scrapers outside the houses. Turn right into River's Street.

STOP 5 ❦ RIVER'S STREET

FOR A LONG TIME RIVER'S STREET MARKED THE NORTHERN LIMIT OF GEORGIAN BATH. ITS ATTRACTIVE, EXPENSIVE HOUSES (SOME WITH DECORATIVE VENETIAN WINDOWS AND TORCH-snuffers at the door still visible) are only yards from the Assembly Rooms. John Wood the Younger built this part of the Upper Town in the 1770s specifically to accommodate tourists. In 1798 Christ Church, at the end of River's Street, was built with more than eight hundred seats available for working-class families and servants unable to afford the usual subscriptions. Walking along River's Street today you can see the last remaining signs of smoke pollution on a blackened house; much of Bath's white stone would have looked like this until the mid-twentieth century, when the long cleaning process began.

This was a favourite address of the many elderly, wealthy widows who moved to Bath, one of whom provided Jane with an unexpected inheritance of fifty pounds after her death in January 1806. This was a large enough sum to cover a year's expenses and enable her to replace her worn clothes. We know very little about the generous Mrs. Lillingston, a close friend of the Leigh-Perrots, except that she lived at 10 River's Street, had fallen out with her daughter and nouveau-riche son-in-law over her late husband's will, and might have been remembered by Jane in *Persuasion* where she places Anne's mentor, Lady Russell, in accommodation on River's Street. The exact nature of their acquaintance remains a mystery.

Walk to the eastern end of River's Street into Brunswick Place, which takes you to the steep Lansdown Road and the high raised pavements of Belvedere, where there are some excellent antique textiles shops. Turn right into Camden Crescent.

Bathwick Ferry with Camden Crescent in the background, 1805

STOP 6 ❧ CAMDEN CRESCENT AND LEAVING BATH

Sir Walter had taken a very good house in Camden-place, a lofty, dignified situation, such as becomes
a man of consequence…Their house was undoubtedly the best in Camden-place; their drawing rooms had
many decided advantages…and the superiority was not less in the style of the fitting-up, or the taste of
the furniture. (Persuasion)

SIR WALTER RENTED THE GRANDEST HOUSE IN CAMDEN-PLACE—A CRESCENT WHOSE FOUN-DATIONS WERE SO INSECURE THAT IT WAS LEFT UNFINISHED, WITH AN UNEVEN NUMBER OF houses on each side of the central house. Teetering on the edge of Beacon Hill, the crescent was placed so high above the city that Sir Walter could not help but look down on the whole of Bath society.

Elizabeth was acutely embarrassed at not being able to issue the expected dinner invitation to her sister, Mary Musgrove, because she "could not bear to have the difference of style, the reduction of servants, which a dinner must betray witnessed by those who had always been so inferior to the Elliots." Convincing herself that "we do not profess to give dinners—few people in Bath do," she takes advantage of the grandeur of the two drawing rooms and offers her sister's family "a regular party—small, but most elegant."

For Anne, her final journey in the novel to Camden Crescent could not have been happier. Walking with Captain Wentworth along the raised pavement of Belmont and onto Belvedere towards her father's house, she was content at last. Earlier a declaration of love contained in a letter had been hastily pushed into her hand at the Musgroves' lodgings; the subsequent chance meeting in Union Street had resulted in Wentworth being asked to escort her home, and "soon words enough had passed between them to decide their direction towards the comparatively quiet and retired gravel-walk, where…they once again exchanged those feelings and promises which had once before seemed to secure everything, but which had been followed by so many years of division and estrangement."

By the time they reached Camden-place, past actions and misunderstandings had been put behind them and they were "more exquisitely happy, perhaps, in their re-union, than when it had first been projected." Jane allowed Anne a happy ending in Bath—one in which she could look forward to a happy marriage and an escape from her unpleasant family: "Bath offered her a break with the past and the promise of future happiness."

When pain is over; the remembrance of it becomes pleasure. One does not love a place the less for having suffered in it, unless it has been all suffering. (Persuasion)

For Jane there was no happy ending in Bath. Much has been made of her dislike of Bath and of her being too depressed to write. But her nephew and biographer J. E. Austen-Leigh was clear that "depression was not in her nature," and given what we know of her resilient character it seems unlikely that she sank into a five-year depression in the city. We do know that she had unhappy experiences during her time there, especially in the last year, when both her father and dear friend Madame Lefroy died within a month of each other. So it is perhaps not surprising that looking back on the Bath years she described the moment of their departure from the city in summer 1806 as being with "happy feelings of escape."

Jane finally returned to the familiar countryside of Hampshire in 1809. Mrs. Austen, Jane and Cassandra, and their good friend Martha Lloyd moved into Chawton Cottage on Edward's estate. Only then did Jane start writing again in earnest, initially revising old manuscripts from the pre-Bath years and then, encouraged by her first publication, *Sense and Sensibility*, in 1811, a succession of new novels at a rate of one a year. The last, and most reflective and romantic novel, *Persuasion*, was written as her health was declining and published posthumously in 1818. She died on July 18, 1817.

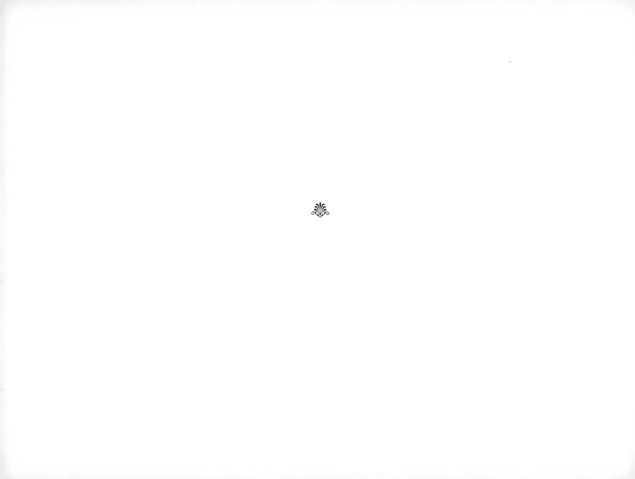

MUSEUMS

ASSEMBLY ROOMS AND MUSEUM OF COSTUME • BENNETT STREET

Tel: +44 (0)1225 477789 • www.museumofcostume.co.uk

Open daily 11am–5pm; closed 4pm during winter

Visitors can wander through the large Ballroom, Octagon Room, Assembly Rooms, Tea Room, and Card Room just as Jane and her family did. On the cloakroom landing is an original ticket to a dress ball held at the Assembly Rooms in January 1803, a time when the Austens might have joined visiting friends for a ball there. The Museum of Costume downstairs houses a collection of historic clothing and accessories and holds regular exhibitions of clothing from different eras. The Fashion Research Centre on the Circus is connected to the museum. Gift shop and bookshop.

BUILDING OF BATH MUSEUM • THE VINEYARDS • PARAGON

Tel: +44 (0)1225 333895 • www.bath-preservation-trust.org.uk/museums/bath/

10:30am–5pm Tuesday–Sunday

This museum of the history of Bath's architecture and interiors traces the development of the city and is housed in the Gothic-style Countess of Huntingdon's Chapel, which dates from the late eighteenth century. Bookshop.

HOLBURNE MUSEUM OF ART ◆ GREAT PULTENEY STREET

Tel: +44 (0) 1225 466669 ◆ www.bath.ac.uk/holburne/

10am–5pm Tuesday–Saturday; from 11am on Sunday

Once the Sydney Hotel, this museum now houses the fine and decorative arts collection of the nineteenth-century ex-naval officer Sir William Holburne, a collection that includes important paintings by the British artists Turner, Kauffmann, and Gainsborough, as well as silver, porcelain, and glass. Gift shop, café, and parking.

JANE AUSTEN CENTRE IN BATH ◆ 40 GAY STREET

Tel: +44 (0) 1225 443000 ◆ janeausten.co.uk

Open daily 10am–5:30pm; 11am–4:30pm November to early March

The Jane Austen Centre contains a permanent exhibition on Jane's time in Bath. The centre also has a café, a gift shop, and a bookshop specializing in books by and about Jane.

THE ROYAL CRESCENT MUSEUM ◆ 1 ROYAL CRESCENT

Tel: +44 (0) 1225 428126 www.bath-preservation-trust.org.uk/museums/no1/

10:30am–5pm Tuesday–Sunday from late February to October; closes 4pm in November

The eighteenth-century room sets in this museum display many objects similar to those used by Jane Austen, as well as contemporary prints and paintings. Gift shop and bookshop.

ROMAN BATHS MUSEUM AND PUMP ROOM (TEA ROOM) ✦ STALL STREET

Tel: +44 (0) 1225 477785 www.romanbaths.co.uk

Open daily 9am–6pm March to June; 9am–9pm July to August; 9:30am–4:30pm November to February

The Baths are now a museum where visitors can see the steaming sulphurous water supplied by natural springs, as well as mosaic floors and the remains of the Roman Baths. The vast Pump Room, a light, airy room lined with tall windows overlooking the Abbey Churchyard, is now used as a restaurant. Visitors can sample the spa water, which contains forty-three minerals, from the elegant pump fountain. There are two sedan chairs displayed, along with portraits of famous Bath residents.

VICTORIA ART GALLERY ✦ BRIDGE STREET

Tel: +44 (0) 1225 477233 ✦ www.victoriagal.org.uk ✦ 10am–5pm Tuesday–Saturday, 2pm–5pm Sunday

This museum houses the region's permanent collection of British and European art from the seventeenth century to the present, including decorative arts and prints from the Regency period. Regular exhibitions throughout the year.

WILLIAM HERSCHEL MUSEUM ✦ 19 NEW KING STREET

Tel: +44 (0) 1225 446865 ✦ www.bath-preservation-trust.org.uk/museums/herschel/
1pm–5pm; weekends from 11am; closed Wednesday

A delightful small Georgian house and garden restored to resemble the time when Sir William Herschel lived there. He moved to Bath from Germany in 1766 and worked initially as a musician, playing the organ part in Handel's *Messiah* at his debut at the fashionable Octagon Chapel. He later became musical director at the Assembly Rooms. Herschel was interested in astronomy, and in March 1781 he and his sister Caroline discovered the planet Uranus. He was made Astronomer Royal the following year by King George III. Shop.

OUTSIDE BATH

JANE AUSTEN'S HOUSE, CHAWTON • CHAWTON, ALTON, HAMPSHIRE
Tel: +44 (0) 1420 83262 • www.jane-austens-house-museum.org.uk • Check opening hours before visiting
This comfortable cottage in the village of Chawton was once owned by Jane Austen's brother Edward. It is a two-hour drive from Bath through lovely countryside, passing near Salisbury Cathedral. Jane lived here with her mother, sister, and a family friend, Martha Lloyd, from 1809–1817. It is now converted into a simply designed museum of the author's life, work, and family. Rooms contain original furniture and objects that belonged to the Austens, such as miniatures and mourning brooches. Gift shop and bookshop.

CAFÉS AND RESTAURANTS

ROYAL CRESCENT HOTEL TEAROOM • 16 ROYAL CRESCENT

Tel. +44 (0) 1225 823333 • www.royalcrescent.co.uk

Lunch 12:30pm–2:30pm; tea 3:30pm–5pm

Enjoy a full English tea of tiny sandwiches, cakes, and Bath buns in the peaceful tea gardens or in the Dower House. Lunch is also available (booking advisable).

ASSEMBLY ROOMS TEAROOM • BARTLETT STREET

Tel. +44 (0) 1225 444477 • Open daily 11am–4:30pm

The original tearoom that Jane frequented are still serving refreshments two hundred years later. Open for morning coffee, lunch, and traditional English teas, including champagne teas, cream teas, and the famous Bath buns.

PUMP ROOMS TEA ROOM • STALL STREET

Tel. +44 (0) 1225 444477 • Open daily 9:30am–4:30pm; in summer, open for dinner

Morning coffee, lunch, and traditional English teas (including champagne teas) are served in the elegant Pump Room, accompanied by musicians and presided over by a full-length sculpture of Beau Nash.

SALLY LUNN'S REFRESHMENT HOUSE AND MUSEUM

Tel: +44 (0) 1225 461634 • Open daily 10am–6pm

One of the oldest houses in Bath, built in 1622 (excavations in the cellar museum reveal remains of Roman and medieval buildings). This bakery has a café serving Sally Lunn buns made from the original recipe.

LIST OF ILLUSTRATIONS

ACKNOWLEDGEMENTS

The author would like to thank Nadia Aguiar and Angela Hederman at the Little Bookroom; the staff of: Bath Reference Library, Bath Record Office, Building of Bath Museum, Victoria Art Gallery, and Shropshire Archives. The following books have proved invaluable: Deirdre le Faye (ed): *Jane Austen's Letters* (3rd Edition, Oxford University Press, 1997); Bath (Pevsner Architectural Guides): Michael Forsyth (Yale University Press, 2003); Jane Austen and Food: Maggie Lane (Hambledon Press, 1995); Becoming Jane Austen: Jon Spence (Hambledon Press, 2003); Jane Austen and Fashion: Penelope Bryde (Excellent Press, 1999); and *Northanger Abbey* and *Persuasion* in the Oxford University Press and Penguin Classics editions.

ABOUT THE AUTHOR

Katharine Reeve is an editor and writer. She is a former Editorial
Director and History Commissioning Editor at Oxford University Press.
She lives in Bath.